MAGIC FAÇADE
THE AUSTIN HOUSE

MAGIC FAÇADE
THE AUSTIN HOUSE

Edited by EUGENE R. GADDIS

Associate Editor, ANN BRANDWEIN

with a Reminiscence by ANGELA LANSBURY

New Photography by GEOFFREY GROSS

WADSWORTH ATHENEUM MUSEUM OF ART

Hartford

Distributed by University Press of New England
Hanover and London

In gratitude to

HELEN GOODWIN AUSTIN, DAVID ETNIER AUSTIN AND SARAH GOODWIN AUSTIN

for their original gift of the Austin House and its collections

to the Wadsworth Atheneum Museum of Art

and

GENEVIEVE HARLOW GOODWIN

whose generosity made possible the restoration and preservation

of the Austin House

This publication appears in conjunction with the exhibition
MAGIC FAÇADE: THE AUSTIN HOUSE
presented by
the Wadsworth Atheneum Museum of Art, Hartford, October 20, 2007–March 9, 2008.

William D. Eppes generously provided the principal funding for this publication.

Design and printing for this book was made possible in part
through generous support from the Felicia Fund and James B. Lyon.

Photography for this book was made possible
in part through a generous grant from Furthermore a program of the J.M. Kaplan Fund.

Additional support came from the Sarah Goodwin Austin Memorial Fund
of the Wadsworth Atheneum Museum of Art.

Copyright © 2007 by the Wadsworth Atheneum Museum of Art
Distributed by UPNE, One Court Street, Lebanon, NH 03766
ISBN no. 0-918333-23-7

Wadsworth Atheneum-Historic House
I. Eugene R. Gaddis
II. David Etnier Austin
III. Richard Guy Wilson
IV. Krystyn Hastings-Silver

Digital Imaging by Allen Phillips
Design by Abigail Sturges
Editing and Index by Indexing Partners
Printed by Hitchcock Printing & Distribution

FRONTISPIECE: The Austin House, 2001.

CONTENTS

PREFACE

COLEMAN H. CASEY

President of the Board of Trustees and Acting Director,
Wadsworth Atheneum Museum of Art

The Austin House was built in 1930 by the Wadsworth Atheneum's legendary director, A. Everett Austin, Jr., and his wife Helen Goodwin Austin. Eighty-six-feet long and eighteen feet deep, the house is in a sense the largest object in the museum's collection. It is also a National Historic Landmark and the Atheneum's official residence. It embodies the history of American modernism and the life and achievements of Chick Austin, who is regarded as one of the most innovative of all American art museum directors.

Each great historic house is unique, but scholars of American art and architecture have consistently maintained that the Austin House stands alone. They have pointed out that it is the only National Historic Landmark that simultaneously demonstrates the rediscovery of baroque art and the emergence of modernism in the international art world during the first third of the twentieth century. It is also the only National Historic Landmark whose social history—its surprising "cast of characters"—represents the confluence of American and European modernists in the United States during the 1930s. For these reasons, as Professor Richard Guy Wilson declares in his illuminating essay, the Austin House is "a national treasure of very great importance."

For many years the Austin House has been the subject of Hartford's most persistent urban legend—that it is only a façade, erected for a variety of fanciful reasons. This book and the exhibition that accompanies it are intended to return the Austin House to its fascinating reality.

Chick Austin was deeply involved with all aspects of the performing arts for most of his life. No one could be more appropriate to raise the curtain on the story of this quintessentially theatrical house than America's best-loved actress, Angela Lansbury. She first met Austin and his family when they moved temporarily to Hollywood in the mid-1940s. Her mother, the actress Moyna Macgill, was a close friend of Austin and later appeared at his summer theater in Windham, New Hampshire, where Miss Lansbury's brothers, Edgar and Bruce, later well-known producers, began their first work in the theater. Miss Lansbury captures Chick Austin's personality and the artistic milieu he created around him with wonderful immediacy. The Wadsworth Atheneum is extremely grateful to her for her participation in this publication and for her membership, for more than two decades, on the Austin House Advisory Council.

Eugene R. Gaddis, the Curator of the Austin House and the Atheneum's William G. DeLana Archivist, provides the principal essay. He tells the story of the Austin House, its creator and his family, based on the research for his biography of Austin, *Magician of the Modern: Chick Austin and the Transformation of the Arts in America*, published by Alfred A. Knopf in 2000. He joined the Atheneum staff in1981 as the museum's first archivist. Soon after discovering Chick Austin's papers, Dr. Gaddis got to know Helen Austin and her two children, Sarah Goodwin Austin and David Etnier Austin, and was closely involved with the Austins' decision to give the house and its collections to the Atheneum. Because of his single-minded vision and tenacity, the restoration of the house has been brought to its rightful and magnificent conclusion.

David Etnier Austin, Chick Austin's son, offers a reminiscence of growing up in the Austin House with his sister Sally, accepting life in rooms that varied in style from baroque to Bauhaus as entirely natural, meeting the leading artists of the

Chick Austin, 1927.

1930s, and being exposed to the artistic exuberance of their father. He also comments on the house from his perspective as an architect.

Richard Guy Wilson, Commonwealth Professor and Chair of the Department of Architectural History at the University of Virginia, provides an essay placing the Austin House in the context of American domestic architecture. Professor Wilson is one of America's best-known architectural historians. He has appeared in numerous television documentaries, such as the PBS series, *America's Castles*. He has been a curator and author for such major exhibitions as *The American Renaissance, 1876–1917*, and *The Machine Age in America, 1918–1941*, which featured the Austin House in its catalogue.

Krystyn Hastings-Silver, the Austin House Restoration Project Manager, and currently the Restoration Project Director at Lyndhurst in Tarrytown, New York, describes the restoration philosophy, the meticulous detective work necessary to ensure authenticity, and the techniques required to recreate the magic of the house and rekindle the spirit of Chick. She organized and supervised all aspects of the restoration from 1998 to 2007.

Photographer Geoffrey Gross, a master of light and atmosphere, has captured the restored interiors of the house, and Abigail Sturges of Sturges Design has once again created a splendid design for an Atheneum publication.

This book would not have been possible without the generosity of William D. Eppes, a lifelong friend of the arts. His own memories of Chick Austin and his appreciation of Austin's significant role in the history of American culture prompted him to suggest the publication and to become its principal sponsor.

We are also extremely grateful to the other sponsors of the book: The Felicia Fund; Furthermore, a Program of the J. M. Kaplan Fund; and James B. Lyon, the first chairman of the Austin House Committee. It has been a particular pleasure to work with The University Press of New England, the distributor of this publication. We express our sincere thanks, as well, to The William and Alice Mortensen Foundation, the sponsor of the accompanying exhibition, also called *Magic Façade: The Austin House*.

Underlying all our work is the generosity of Helen, David, and Sally Austin and their cousin Genevieve Harlow Goodwin who made it possible for the Atheneum to restore and preserve this magical house, which since its completion in 1930 has been so closely linked to the museum.

We hope that those who are introduced to the story of Chick and Helen Austin and the Austin House will gain a deeper understanding of the history of the arts in America as well as an appreciation for the knowledge and passion that carried the Atheneum to the forefront of the museum world.

A REMINISCENCE OF CHICK AUSTIN

ANGELA LANSBURY

The first time I met him, I remember that he was in a pair of old gray slacks, sneakers, a navy blue and red striped shirt open at the neck, his hair disheveled, no hat, and a cigarette hanging out of his mouth—and that was Chick. The inevitable cigarette—because he couldn't stop talking long enough to take it out of his mouth, because his enthusiasm and his joie de vivre were so enormous and so catching!

I was a very young woman at the time, probably eighteen years old, newly arrived in Hollywood—originally from London—with my family. Chick became a friend of mine through my mother Moyna Macgill, who was an actress—very beautiful, and a wonderful comedienne—and they got along like a house on fire. And he became a friend of my brothers, Edgar and Bruce. Though he was quite a bit older than us, he treated us all as his equals, that was the thing. He always came back from the East armed with amazing tales of projects that he was involved with.

Although I didn't visit his Hartford house until the 1970s, I did get to know his homes in Los Angeles, and they left a lasting impression. My education always came from the people I met, their taste, and what they exposed me to, and I was always interested in how you evolve a taste for yourself. Chick bought a first house on Miller Drive, off the Sunset Strip, and that was where he brought some bits and pieces of furniture, I assume from Hartford. He leaned to the baroque, and there was always that feeling about the house—rather Venetian. He loved everything seventeenth and eighteenth century. I think Chick was the person who opened my eyes to the beauty of those great periods of architecture and design. I began to understand and appreciate certain things that he incorporated in his houses—French bergères, sconces, paneling and wall coverings.

It was always an "event" if you went to Chick's house. He was terribly hospitable and warm and generous-hearted. He enjoyed being around a lot of people and would gather an incredible mixture from the world of arts and letters—actors, writers, artists, dancers.

I never quite knew what he wanted to do in Hollywood. He was just this fascinating top that never stopped spinning.

By 1946 Chick had a second house on South Westgate Avenue in Brentwood, and Helen and their children, David and Sally, all moved there from Hartford. Helen was extremely shy, gentle and warm and friendly and sweet—an absolute angel of a woman. She adored Chick and stood behind everything and anything he did.

Chick was like a honey bee. He went around tasting and enjoying everything artistic that appealed to the senses. He had the most subtle antenna, and when he picked up on something that fired up his imagination, he wanted to be involved, wanted to know about it, dip into it, pursue it, and help bring about something original and significant to its conclusion.

He was enormously proud of the Atheneum, and it obviously represented a very large part of his life. He always talked of himself as connected to it. He was not proud in a boastful way, but I think he had a great sense that he had brought about something rather extraordinary there and that what he accomplished future generations would gratefully inherit.

Angela Lansbury, c. 1944.

THE STAGE-SET HOUSE

EUGENE R. GADDIS

William G. DeLana Archivist and Curator of the Austin House
Wadsworth Atheneum Museum of Art

On the morning of Tuesday, December 16, 1930, Chick Austin and his wife Helen opened their newly completed home in Hartford, Connecticut, to visitors. He was the dashing Harvard-trained director of the city's venerable Wadsworth Atheneum, a sedate repository of art that he was rapidly transforming into one of the country's most vibrant and forward-looking museums. She was the quietly refined eighth-generation descendant of Hartford's preeminent founding family, the Goodwins; but unlike many of her relatives, she delighted in her husband's provocative creativity. The showing of their house was presented as a one-day exhibition of furniture and decorative arts under the auspices of the Atheneum; and for twelve hours, the glamorous couple gave tours to more than four hundred members of the museum. Two days later, Chick Austin celebrated his thirtieth birthday.[1]

At first glance, all that visitors to 130 Scarborough Street could see as they looked beyond a low hedge and across a sweeping wintry lawn, was a flat eighty-six-foot-long Palladian façade. The house was modeled on a sixteenth-century villa that Chick and Helen had seen along the Brenta River near Venice during their wedding trip the previous summer, but their version was less a copy than a pastiche. Instead of brick and stucco, it was constructed of horizontal pine boards, painted white. Its tall pilasters were only a few inches deep; its Ionic capitals were more streamlined than any baroque architect would have imagined, or wanted; and the four false windows that disrupted the symmetry of the façade were clearly the product of an irreverent twentieth-century mind. It had a cool elegance. It also had a strangely two-dimensional quality, as if it were not quite real—an impression that was reinforced on closer inspection. The Austins' house was only eighteen feet deep.

Stepping through the front door, visitors seemed to have left the insurance capital of the world and entered what appeared to be a European villa of some antiquity. The entry hall—its curved walls painted a sandy beige—extended two stories upward to a white, lighted dome. The stone floor was travertine, a material favored by both Italian Renaissance architects and modernist builders. A graceful staircase with a dark blue carpet curved upward along the wall opposite the front door. Dominating the entry was a life-size seventeenth-century Italian painted and gilded wooden sculpture of Saint Luke, the patron saint of artists and physicians, made in Antwerp, holding his gospel and standing on a weathered black pedestal. The saint was installed halfway up the wall above the stairs as if he were floating. Below the staircase, from the same period, was a Bohemian wooden sculpture of a horse and a rider holding a spear, with a diminutive dragon attached to the horse's feet. This seemingly grand entrance hall was an exercise in illusion, for the first tread of the staircase was a scant four feet from the front door and the house ended just two yards behind the curved wall.

A short passage with a rose carpet led to the right. Its walls were hung with an eighteenth-century red and cream French toile depicting Chinese musicians with quaint instruments processing toward exotic pavilions. Against one wall was an old Venetian door painted in faded blues and greens and inset with a wavy mirror distorting one's reflection, with the date 1723 at the top of the frame, along with a Latin phrase invoking God's blessing on those who lived in the house. Across from it was a modern door to a telephone closet.

Small double doors opened into a narrow music room, where the visitors could appreciate the true depth of the house because the space extended the full

RIGHT 130 Scarborough Street, December 1930.

BELOW *The Hartford Times* heralds the Austin House, March 15, 1930.

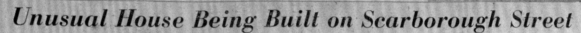

SECOND SECTION
PAGE TWENTY-FIVE
SATURDAY, MARCH 15, 1930.

The Hartford Time

West Hartford Park, Town and Ceme
New Layout Meets With Comme

PALLADIAN HOUSE REPRODUCED HERE

Mr. and Mrs. A. Everett Austin, Jr., Building New Home at No. 130 Scarborough St.

UNIQUE IN CONSTRUCTION

Residence Is Eighteen Feet Wide by Eighty-six Feet Long; Unusual Features.

One of the most interesting and unusual residences in Hartford is being built at No. 130 Scarborough street by A. Everett Austin, jr., director of the Wadsworth Atheneum, and Mrs. Austin. Patterned after a Palladian house of the sixteenth century, it is eighteen feet wide by eighty-six feet long. The original house is said by many to be the source of all Colonial architecture. Palladio's pupils and followers having carried the style of architecture down through the years to the colonists. Even the setting of Mr. Austin's new house is similar in many respects to that of the original mansion. The Palladian house is located on the Brenta river, near Venice, the river flowing at the rest of the building. The Hartford house is located on the Park river, which winds itself past the rear and at the feet of Mr. Austin's property. The Brenta river is only slightly larger than a Hartford stream.

Mr. French's Design

The Hartford house designed by Leigh French, jr., of New York, and is being built by the Allyn Wadhams company, general contractors, is two stories high, and when finished will have a plain wood exterior, the boards being laid flush with each other. The color has not yet been definitely decided upon. The roof will be of cedar shingles.

The first floor rooms will be eleven feet high, while the second floor rooms will be eight feet high. A terrace will extend along the front of the house, with another at the rear.

Everything in the lines of the house is perfectly symmetrical. Each window on one side is directly opposite a window or door on the other side, and where there is a window is opposite a door, it is designed to give the effect of a window. The windows, incidentally, are large, and with the narrowness of the house—one room in width—extraordinarily good ventilation is secured. The outstanding point of architecture, as one approaches this house, is the portico with four tall pillars at the entrance.

Circular Entrance Hall

The entrance hall of Mr. Austin's

Unusual House Being Built on Scarborough Street

KITCHEN | PANTRY | DINING·ROOM | GALLERY | LAV. | FOYER | LIVING ROOM
ENTRANCE HALL

HOUSE CLEANING MAY BE LIGHTENED

Home Demonstration Agent Gives

NORTH OXFORD STREET RESIDENCE SOLD

The attractive residence at No. 157 North Oxford street was sold this week by Dr. D. B. Cochran to Leroy S. Purrington of the Fuller Brush company. The deal was negotiated through the agency of Hart, Kneeland and Poindexter, real estate agents. The house contains ten rooms, two baths, and a two-car garage. Dr. Cochran is moving into his new residence recently completed on Golf road.

WEEK'S BUILDING AWARDS.

Contracts for building and engineering projects in New England awarded during the week ended March 11, amounted to $4,499,900, according to the F. W. Dodge corporation. This amount was $96,000 more than the average of the previous weeks this year, but approximately $2,200,000 less than the value of the contracts awarded during the corresponding week last year.

BLOOMFIELD LAND IS SOLD.

Julius F. Huss of West Hartford has bought from eight to ten acres of land in Bloomfield near the Simsbury town line, it was announced yesterday by the Goeben Realty company of West Hartford, who negotiated the sale. The former owners were John M. and Raymond A. Porteus. It is understood that Mr. Huss bought the property as an investment.

WINDING STREETS WILL BE FEATURE

Parkways and Other Beautifying Features Also Included in West Hartford Plans.

FINE NEW DEVELOPMENT

Several Others That Have Given Town Its Attractiveness Have Been Laid Out.

The preliminary hearing on the proposed layout by the West Hartford park, town plan, and cemetery commission, held this week, wherein the commission has proposed winding streets, parkways, and other beautifying features not usually found in development plans, has caused a good deal of discussion among property owners and developers. The discussion, however, has almost all been of a commendatory nature, and the people of West Hartford, to all outward appearances, appreciate to the fullest the attempt of the commission to make future West Hartford residential developments as beautiful and attractive as possible.

Proposed Layout.

The proposed layout of the plan commission is not the first development to be laid out in this manner. Several others, almost as large, have been planned and the layouts carried out by real estate developers without aid from the commission until they were ready for acceptance by the

This is the first time, as far as can be learned, that the park, town and cemetery commission has ever gone ahead on its own initiative and proposed a layout of streets for a tract of property. It was done in the nature of an experiment, according to members of the commission, and approval by the property owners indicated its success.

Whether the town plan commission will suggest layouts for their streets has not been decided. It was intimated this week that property owners in the future have to get together and request the commission to act, if the layout is made.

Developments in Past.

In all large development projects in the past, the realtors or developers have gone to the expense of having the land surveyed, and then laying out the streets as they saw fit, subject to the approval of the commission, looking back over a period of the last few years, few mistakes have been made according to a town official, as each separate development has been laid out with little or no regard to the future layout of an adjacent development might be. What future takes have been made, is to said to be serious in business areas.

AMONG THOSE PRES-ENT—In the gather-ing of representative Hart-ford and Middletown citizens aboard the Steamer Middletown on her maiden trip of the season May 27, The Courant camera noted Miss Helen Goodwin and A. Everett Austin, director of the Morgan Memorial, this city. The above snap was made as the steamer was leaving the Hartford dock at the foot of State Street.   Courant Photos

Helen Goodwin and Chick Austin aboard the steamer *Middletown* on the Connecticut River, May 27, 1929.

eighteen feet with a window on either end. Its canvas walls were painted a soft tawny gold and its woodwork a rich caramel. The beadwork of all the moldings was lightly streaked with thin lines of Chinese red, like threads tying the room together. The color picked up the tones in four framed eighteenth-century Venetian wall panels of darkening gold silk, each picturing one or two faint Chinese figures with suggestions of foliage. Having run out of wall space, Austin had attached a fifth panel to the ceiling. Set into the long wall across from the entrance to the living room was a framed mirror of small square sections. On either side of a cabinet under the mirror were two extravagantly carved and painted side chairs in a chinoiserie style by Michael Angelo Pergolesi, the celebrated eighteenth-century Italian designer of furniture and decorative objects.

Entry to the living room was under a sinuous archway. Huge carved eighteenth-century doors, taken from a German or French armoire, opened into the room like two rococo wings. This space was two steps below the central part of the house, so that when arriving for cocktails or dinner, one could look out over the other guests before making an entrance, like an actor stepping down from a stage. An eleven-foot ceiling made the room appear larger than it was in reality. Covering the walls were eight oversize Italian canvas panels painted in Turin about 1730, the most prominent of them copied from a picture by Claude Lorraine.[2] They served as theatrical backdrops for the room, presenting classical harbor scenes, stormy seascapes, and figures in seventeenth-century costumes—inviting guests to see themselves, at least while the party lasted, as inhabitants of a grander, more heroic world. To set off the panels, Austin had painted the walls a dark blue-green, which suggested a mixture of the colors in the turbulent skies and seas. Complementing these tones was the same dusty rose wall-to-wall carpeting found in the music room, made of hand-sewn strips. Broadloom was available, but Austin wished to recall an earlier time and avoid any association with middle-class décor. Curtains of a simple design, in a misty rose silk taffeta, provided luxury without distracting the eye from the panels. To enhance the romantic effect, soft ambient lighting came from sconces and lamps, fitted with the newly available frosted bulbs. No chandelier was present to cast unflattering shadows from above.

The colors on all the walls and ceilings—and each ceiling was a different color—were unique to the house because Chick Austin mixed them himself. An artist from childhood, he had refined his visual acuity at Harvard's Fogg Art Museum and throughout Europe to such a degree that he was known among his peers as having one of the finest eyes of his generation. In addition to the formidable connoisseurship he demonstrated as director of a fine arts institution, his talent for interior decoration was something he would exercise all his life, whether for his many houses, the two art museums he headed, or the three theaters for which

ABOVE Front hall, 1930.   BELOW Living room, 1930.   ABOVE Music room, `1930, .   BELOW Living room, 1930.

Dining room, 1930.

Dining room, 1930.

he acted as producer. One friend who watched him creating colors in later years remembered him rapidly squeezing tubes of various shades into a bucket of a white base paint until he got exactly what he wanted. "He loved colors that had no name," she said. "They were such blends. Everything was a game. If you saw green, and you saw blue, that's the way he wanted it."[3]

From the living room visitors could walk back up to the music room and down a rear passage painted in two shades of yellow. Proceeding to the end of the hall, through a set of small double doors, they entered the dining room, which like the living room was two steps below. This was the most luxurious space of all. Across the room on the north wall, was an enormous boiserie, or wooden alcove, in the rococo style, with doors at either side and embellished with carved flowers, leaves, tendrils, and cherubs—its original paint and gold gilt only faintly visible. The other walls were covered in a worn but shimmering antique blue-green silk brocatelle, woven in a baroque pattern, with matching curtains for the front window and the French doors that led to the rear terrace. Austin had painted the wide crown molding antique white to set the alcove off as an object. The ceiling was gray so that the

eye would not be distracted from the intricate surfaces of woodwork and fabric. A simple mahogany Louis XVI table that could be extended to seat twelve stood in the center of the room, along with a few caned chairs in the more ornamental Louis XV style. As in the living room, there was no chandelier. Light came from lunettes over the doors in the alcove, rococo sconces, and candles. The room was so alluring that guests would often say that they were going to Chick Austin's house to dine in the "blue lagoon."

The first floor conjured up a fantasy world of the eighteenth century, in which decorative design had reached a level of exquisite, graceful elegance, aged by two hundred years into a faded grandeur. Despite his modernism, Austin's romantic temperament drew him to that period, and he never stopped buying rococo furniture, fabrics, pictures and decorative objects. As he later wrote of the style, "the utmost richness of texture was attained by all of the arts on a scale which, since it was always intimate, could never err on the side of pomposity or pretension." He admitted that "no profound truth was perhaps expressed by the art of the Rococo," but "a model of tremendous refinement of taste was created for the future."[4]

Helen Austin's dressing room, 1930.

Helen Austin's dressing room, 1930.

When visitors returned to the entry hall and climbed the stairs to the second floor, they walked through the master bedroom, which was an architecturally modern space decorated in gray and green. (It would soon be changed to a space with pale peach-pink walls, beige woodwork and a light blue ceiling. These unlikely colors were chosen to complement the curtains and bed hangings done in a classic pink, beige, blue and purple Alsatian fabric with flowers and peacocks.) Visitors then entered a short passage with walls covered with a pale gray-green Art Deco fabric of cotton and rayon, called "Broken Sticks," made by the French weaver Hélène Henry. This led to Helen Austin's dressing room. And there they entered the twentieth century with a jolt.

Sleek and stark, with a black floor of sheet linoleum polished to a high gloss, the room featured walls of different colors, five mirrors, German chromium tubular lights, and tubular steel furniture by Marcel Breuer, upholstered in gray-blue *Eisengarn*, or "iron yarn." The space was modeled primarily on the dressing room of Bauhaus founder Walter Gropius in the Master's House at the famous school of design in Dessau, Germany, which Gropius had designed with Breuer, his colleague at the

Bauhaus. To complement the Breuer furniture in Helen's dressing room, Austin had borrowed a chromium chair and a chaise longue by architect Le Corbusier from a friend at the Museum of Modern Art. In an interview with the *Courant* two months later, Austin declared that the best of modern design "is genuinely in keeping with the spirit of the age. . . . So are the electric light fixtures, made to suggest electricity, rather than gas or candles, and of plain finish, such as a machine would naturally turn out, rather than an imitation of hand craftsmanship."[5]

The colors of the walls were not those generally used in Bauhaus interiors, but Austin had absolute confidence in his taste and thought nothing of imbuing the sometimes regimented architecture of the Bauhaus with colors of his own invention. One wall was gray-blue, one cream, one beige, and one a deep cocoa. Each plane facing the same direction, including the interiors of the cabinets and the closets, was painted the same color, including jet-black for the shelves. As Austin told the *Hartford Times*, "the difference in color is very restful as it follows the natural values of light. Thus the wall opposite the principal windows is finished in a light color, while the first wall, naturally in the shadow, is done in a dark color."[6] Austin's acute

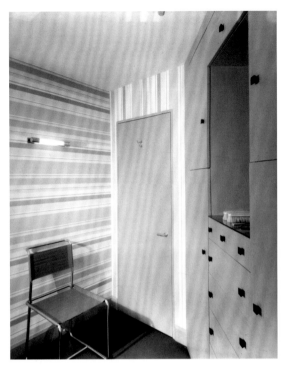

Chick Austin's
dressing room, 1930.

ABOVE Guest bedroom, 1930.   BELOW Basement "rumpus room," 1930.

Chick Austin's
bathroom, 1930.

awareness of surface textures in the baroque-rococo style applied equally to the textures of modern spaces. He knew that without the distraction of ornament, the subtle interplay of surface and color became even more critical to the success and interest of modern design.

Chick's dressing room, reached through another door in the bedroom, was smaller, but in the same style as Helen's, with the same light fixtures and glossy black linoleum. In the outer room, furnished with a Breuer chair, Austin had painted one wall cream and covered another with wallpaper of multicolored horizontal and vertical stripes. His bathroom, its walls painted blue-green, beige, and brown, and its ceiling a lighter brown, was remarkable for a black toilet, a black tub fitted with a sheet of stainless steel on the side, and a standing stainless steel wash basin. Above the tub, two glass shelves projected from the wall, appearing as floating geometric planes. On the wall near the sink, Chick later mounted a round aluminum and steel shaving mirror by Bauhaus designer Marianne Brandt.

Visitors could see one other area on the second floor, a guest room decorated in the much less austere Art Deco aesthetic, introduced five years earlier in Paris at the widely influential *Exposition Internationale des Arts Décoratifs et Industriels Modernes*. This room featured wallpaper of abstract shapes in lime and lemon and curving furniture by German designer Bruno Paul, painted in pale green enamel and silver. A final variation on modern designs that were diametrically opposed could be found in the basement bar, known by Chick's friends in those Prohibition days as "the rumpus room." This space combined Bauhaus-style walls of different colors with a hanging bed by Art Deco designer Pierre Charreau, which Chick had installed in his bachelor apartment a year after he came to Hartford.

It was the two dressing rooms, however, that made the most impact. They were among the very first examples of this radically new design to be found in America. It is unlikely that any of those escorted through them in December 1930 had ever previously beheld such spaces in person. The style of these rooms was so ultra-modern that two years would pass before it was codified by the Museum of Modern Art in a touring exhibition, created by Chick's close friends from Harvard, Henry-Russell Hitchcock and Philip Johnson: *Modern Architecture: International Style*, whose third venue was the Atheneum.

Taken as a whole, the house was, in effect, Chick Austin's stage set for the theater of his life. It was a reflection of his personal taste as well as his purposes as the director of an art museum. Helen shared his artistic interests whole-heartedly, and she gladly deferred to his judgment on questions of color and design.

There had been such public interest in the house that four days earlier the *Hartford Courant* had devoted a rotogravure section of its Sunday edition to the house and its interiors. After the day-long tour, both of Hartford's newspapers published arti-

The Hartford Courant,
December 17, 1930.

cles describing it. The *Hartford Times* singled out the chair and chaise lounge in Helen's dressing room, eager to inform its readers that they were the only examples of Le Corbusier's work in America.[7] The *Courant* reported that "visitors examined the effect of combining an experimental contemporary style with traditional eighteenth century forms in decorations and furniture. They found the exterior of this setting as unusual as the interiors. . . . " The paper declared that "the furnishings of this magnificent dwelling" constituted a "unique exhibition of decorative arts."[8]

The house was not universally applauded. Austin's neighbors, several of them members of the museum's board, who had built solid, respectable neo-colonial or Tudor-revival houses on Scarborough Street in the 1920s, dubbed the miniature villa "the pasteboard palace." The lawyer across the street in his big Georgian-style brick edifice called it "an excrescence."[9] And an Atheneum trustee who lived two blocks away was known to have waved a hand dismissively toward it as he drove by, uttering in disgust: *That – Chick – Austin.*"[10]

Austin was well aware that some members of the Hartford establishment already viewed his dramatic persona and his unabashed promotion of all things modern with skepticism. But with his self-assurance, he almost always responded to the rumblings of the older generation with amusement. When an out-of-town friend asked him about the house soon after it was built, Austin responded with characteristically double-edged wit: "Oh, the house is just like me—all façade."[11]

Austin's remark was prophetic, for over the following decades, a widespread and persistent mythology developed in Hartford around his architectural statement. It was "the fake house," "the cardboard house," a movie set from the 1920s that had never been taken down. It hid a water tower, or electrical equipment, that for some unexplained reason had to occupy a space in the middle of one of Hartford's most expensive pieces of real estate. Or it was nothing more than a wooden flat in front of a much smaller house, erected by the owner to avoid the embarrassment of living among the grander homes on the street.

The house was of course substantial enough to be filled during its early years with more artistic effervescence than any other house in Hartford since the 1870s when Samuel Clemens built his own flamboyant mansion on nearby Farmington Avenue. The Austins' house became a gathering place for an astonishing number of leading figures in the international art world—Alexander Calder, Salvador Dali, George Balanchine, Gertrude Stein, Marguerite Yourcenar, Le Corbusier, Walter Gropius, Philip Johnson, Buckminster Fuller, Cecil Beaton, Agnes de Mille, Martha Graham, Alwyn Nikolais, Aaron Copland, Virgil Thomson, Lincoln Kirstein, Lotte Lenya and Kurt Weill. They came to take part in Chick's activities and programs at the Atheneum that led to a cultural flowering so vivid that in 1936 a headline in the theatrical newspaper *Variety* actually called Hartford "America's New Salzburg."[12] And Austin emerged as one of the country's most influential champions of the two extremes of art reflected in his house, the baroque and the modern.

Austin himself was compulsively creative. He was a teacher, a painter, an actor, a designer of sets and costumes, a superb cook, and a stage magician of professional quality. But it was as a connoisseur, an impresario and a participant in all the arts that he became, in the words of Virgil Thomson, "a whole cultural movement in one man."[13]

A. Everett Austin, Jr., was born on December 18, 1900, in Brookline, Massachusetts. His mother, Laura Etnier Austin, a well-educated woman from rural Pennsylvania, had inherited money from her rich Uncle John Morrison in 1890, when

Six-year-old Everett with his mother, 1907.

she was twenty-six. She turned herself into an "heiress" with aristocratic vowels in all the wrong places, and went off in 1896 with her sister Virginia on a grand tour of Europe. There she met Dr. Arthur Everett Austin, a man of few words from a long line of Maine farmers, who had attended Bowdoin College and Harvard Medical School. On leave from the Tufts Medical School faculty and pursuing advanced medical studies in Berlin, he seemed promising as the father of a child. Laura kept in touch. They were married in a New York hotel in 1899.

Soon after Everett was born, Laura began creating the proper background for her "Boy Dear," as she addressed him even after he became a museum director. In 1901 she built a substantial summer cottage in South Harpswell, on the Maine coast. In 1904 Arthur decided to return to Europe for a further year's study, this time in Vienna. While he worked on medicine, Laura and her sister, who came along with the marriage, traveled through Europe with three-year-old Everett, visiting churches, palaces, and museums. In 1909 the Austins went to live in Dresden for additional medical studies. Everett learned to speak and write German at school, made miniature theater sets, and performed his own version of Wagner's *Flying Dutchman* for his friends. In 1910 they were in Paris, where the boy became proficient in French at a school on the rue de la Grande Armée and entertained his classmates as "Professor Marvel" with the first of his magic shows. In Switzerland, in the summer of 1912, while studying at the Institut de Jeunes Gens near Lausanne, Everett took up painting. Laura encouraged her clever son in all his artistic pursuits.

Meanwhile, the family moved to a large post-Civil War townhouse at 110 Marlborough Street in Boston's Back Bay, and Everett was sent to the exclusive Noble & Greenough School. Laura made certain that he was always dressed in the best custom-tailored clothes. Everett soon acquired the nickname "Chick" from his friends because of his diminutive size and impish nature. In 1913 Laura bought an estate in Windham, New Hampshire, with three houses and a barn overlooking Cobbett's Pond, so that like many of his more well-born classmates, her boy could have a country place to retreat to on weekends and during the summer when the family was not in Maine.

Obsessed with genealogy, she claimed that she and Everett were descended from Norse kings, Scottish chieftains, French nobility, and at least one pope. Deciding that her mother's family, the Morrisons, was the noblest of them all, she ordered engraved stationery and bookplates with the Morrison crest for her son, and had signet rings made for the two of them, hers in gold, his in platinum, which he wore for the rest of his life.

In 1918, after a second senior year at Andover, Chick entered Harvard with a concentration in fine arts and quickly plunged into the world of cocktails, cigarettes, debutant balls, musical shows, and the general attractions of what he later described

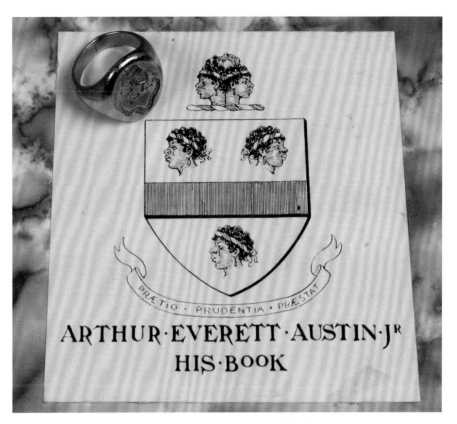

Chick Austin's signet ring and bookplate with the Morrison family crest.

as "Boston and red paint."[14] His transcript was covered with warnings about not appearing for classes and examinations, and he had to repeat his freshman year. It was not until the fall of 1921, when he took two courses by America's most distinguished Egyptologist, George Reisner, that Chick became truly motivated. He was entranced with Egyptian art and history, applied himself, and earned his first two A's at Harvard.

Recognizing his student's potential, Reisner invited him to spend the next season as his assistant in Egypt and the Sudan. Accompanied by his mother, Chick sailed for Egypt in September 1922, stopping in England, France and Italy along the way. In Florence he saw the ground-breaking exhibition of Italian baroque painting, *Pittura Italiana del Seicento e del Settecento*. With more than a thousand pictures, the show was a revelation to the art world. In England, it prompted the "dandy-aesthetes" at Oxford, who loved its voluptuous excess, to embrace the baroque, as they had the *commedia dell' arte* and Serge Diaghilev's Ballets Russes.

Chick Austin at Giza, Egypt, 1922.

Among them was Sacheverell Sitwell, who published his seminal monograph *Southern Baroque Art* in 1924. This introduced a whole generation to the delights of baroque architecture and painting, which had been denigrated by art critics for a century as too theatrical, too sensual, and degenerate. Chick called Sitwell's book and its sequels the foundation of his aesthetic taste.[15]

Chick arrived at the Harvard Camp at Giza in October 1922, just a month before Howard Carter discovered King Tutankamen's tomb in the Valley of the Kings, which added to Chick's excitement. He took up painting again beside the pyramids and, to set the scene, played Rimsky-Korsakov's *Sheherezade* every night on a wind-up gramophone. The party, including his mother, traveled a thousand miles up the Nile to the ruins of Meroë, where Chick learned to settle down and work to the exacting standards of one of the world's great archaeologists. Reisner's team opened about 800 tombs that season, and in recovering objects that had not been seen since they were created, two or three thousand years earlier, Chick began to see that all art, when it is looked at with the knowledge of how it was made, becomes contemporary art.

Before returning to Harvard, he spent several months touring Europe with his mother. In June of 1924, in Paris, he met up with Paul Sachs, one of his art history professors and the Associate Director of the Fogg Art Museum, whose course in museum studies was the first of its kind in the United States. Sachs took him to the Ballets Russes for the first time, and he saw two works by Stravinsky, *Pulcinella* and *Les Noces*. He returned every year for two weeks of the Russian Ballet in London until Diaghilev's death in 1929. This immersion in one of the greatest artistic collaborations of all time—which Chick called "the most intense emotional experience of my life"—along with his own deeply theatrical nature, made him a leader in opening the doors of American museums to the performing arts.[16]

Back in Cambridge in 1924, Chick finished up his undergraduate career by taking the one course taught by the director of the Fogg, Edward Forbes—"Methods and Processes of Italian Painting," also known as the "the egg and plaster course," in which students learned connoisseurship by practicing the techniques of the Renaissance painters. Chick did so well that Forbes asked him to be his teaching assistant for the next three years. To prepare him, Forbes sent Chick to study with one of Italy's most accomplished forgers, Federigo Ioni, in Siena, where he also learned his fourth language. When he returned to Harvard, he completed his formal education with Sachs's invaluable museum course. The Fogg was America's only training ground for connoisseurship and museum studies, and from Forbes and Sachs Chick absorbed the conviction that promoting the knowledge and understanding of art was one of the noblest goals of American education.

Early in 1927 Forbes and Sachs were approached by Charles A. Goodwin, the president of the Wadsworth Atheneum, to recommend a young man to become the

The Wadsworth Atheneum, c. 1920.

first professionally trained director of the museum. They both named Chick as the best candidate for the job. The Atheneum had at that time half a million dollars in one fund, rapidly earning interest, for the construction of a new building, and the imminent bequest of just over a million in another fund restricted to buying choice paintings. With these two plums dangling before him, Chick accepted the position of director, beginning in October, at an annual salary of $3500. At almost the same time, he accepted an offer from the president of Trinity College to start the school's art history department by teaching one course each semester, which he continued for the next fifteen years, becoming a kind of pied piper to generations of students. He was twenty-six and a very cosmopolitan young man.

With irrepressible energy, Austin immediately set out to turn America's oldest public art museum into its most advanced. The Atheneum was founded in 1842 by Daniel Wadsworth, a Hartford benefactor and an early patron of the arts in America. It was an accretion of buildings that covered a city block, known in the 1920s for its American history paintings, American landscapes of the Hudson River

School, the Pierpont Morgan Collection of antiquities and European decorative objects, and the unrivalled Wallace Nutting collection of "Pilgrim century" furniture and household utensils. There were also cases of coins and military medals and rooms full of butterflies and stuffed birds. Early on, Chick met Francis Goodwin II, the insurance agent for the museum, his future brother-in-law and later the founder of the Hartford Symphony, who remarked conversationally that the museum had "a pretty good plant." "Yes," Austin retorted, "it's a pretty good plant. The only thing we need to do now is find something to put in it."[17]

During his seventeen-year tenure, Austin virtually created both the European Old Master and the modernist collections at the Atheneum, buying perceptively in both areas. He acquired hundreds of works by painters ranging from Fra Angelico and Piero di Cosimo to Lucas Cranach, Murillo, Tintoretto, Strozzi, Magnasco, Valdés Leal, Le Nain, Claude Lorraine, Poussin, Rubens, Sweerts, Meléndez, Tiepolo, Guardi, Bellotto, Chardin, Greuze, Goya, Daumier, Corot, Degas, and Gauguin. He was the first American museum director to acquire works by artists such

Piero di Cosimo, 1462–1522.
The Finding of Vulcan on Lemnos, c. 1490.

Oil and tempera on canvas, 61 x 68¼ inches.
Purchased 1932.

Michael Sweerts, 1618–1664.
Boy with Hat, c. 1660.

Oil on canvas, 14⅛ x 11⅝ inches.
 Purchased 1940.

Workshop of Fra Angelico, 1418–1455.
Head of an Angel, c.1440.

Tempera and oil on panel, 6⅞ x 5½ inches.
Purchased 1928.

Michelangelo Merisi da Caravaggio,
1571–1610.

Ecstasy of Saint Francis, c. 1594.
Oil on canvas, 37 x 51 inches.
Purchased 1943.

Bernardo Strozzi, 1581/2–1644.
Saint Catherine of Alexandria, c. 1610–1615.

Oil on canvas, 69⅛ x 48½ inches. Purchased 1931.

Paul Gauguin, 1848–1903.
Nirvana: Portrait Meyer de Haan,
c. 1889–1890.

Gouache on silk or linen with
touches of pencil and gold leaf,
8¼ x 11⅜ inches. Purchased 1943.

William Harnett, 1848–1892.
The Faithful Colt, 1890.

Oil on canvas, 22⅛ x 18½ inches.
Purchased 1935.

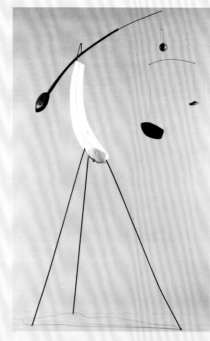

Alexander Calder, 1898–1976.
The Praying Mantis, 1936.

Wood rod, wire, string, and paint,
78 x 51 x 40 inches. © Calder
Foundation, New York / Artists Rights
Society (ARS), New York. Purchased
1938.

Joan Miró, 1893–1983.
Painting, 1933.

Oil on canvas, 54⅜ x 64½ inches.
© 2007 Successió Miró / Artists Rights
Society (ARS), New York / ADAGP, Paris.
Purchased 1934.

Edward Hopper,
1882–1967.
*Captain Strout's
House, Portland
Head*, 1927.

Watercolor on paper,
14 x 20 inches.
Purchased 1928.

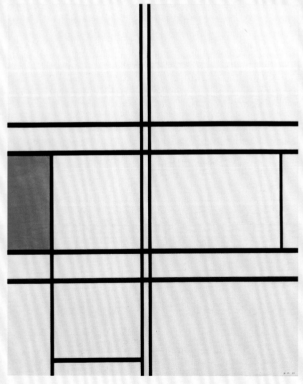

Piet Mondrian,
1872–1944.
*Composition (No IV)
Blanc Bleu* 1934/35
*Composition in Blue
and White*, 1935.

Oil on canvas,
41 x 38 inches. © 2007
Mondrian / Holtzman Trust
c/o HCR International VA.
Purchased 1936.

Salvador Dalí, 1904–1989.
Apparition of a Face and a Fruit Dish on a Beach, 1938.

Oil on canvas, 45 x 56⅝ inches.
© 2007 Salvador Dali, Gala-Salvador Dali Foundation /
Artists Rights Society (ARS), New York. Purchased 1939.

Joseph Cornell,
American, 1903–1972.
Soap Bubble Set, 1936.

Mixed media; 15¾ x 14¼
inches. Art © The Joseph and
Robert Cornell Memorial
Foundation / Licensed by
VAGA, New York, NY.
Purchased 1938.

Max Ernst, 1891–1976.
Europe After the Rain,
1940–1942.

Oil on canvas, 21⁹⁄₁₆ x 58³⁄₁₆
inches. © 2007 Artists Rights
Society (ARS), New York /
ADAGP, Paris. Purchased
1942.

as Caravaggio, William Harnett, Salvador Dali, Joan Miró, Piet Mondrian, and Joseph Cornell, and made early purchases of watercolors by Edward Hopper to whom he gave his first solo museum exhibition. Among the many other twentieth-century masters whose works he bought before they were well known were Giorgio de Chirico, Alexander Calder, Charles Demuth, Jean Arp, Balthus, Paul Klee, Yves Tanguy, and Max Ernst.

But Chick also liked to have fun. In April 1928, six months after he arrived, he produced the museum's first ball, the Venetian Fête, in which the upper echelon of Hartford society was invited to dress in silks and satins as eighteenth-century Venetian nobles and characters from the *commedia dell'arte*. They all paraded through the museum's Tapestry Hall, which Chick had decorated with theatrical flats of Venice that he had painted himself and illuminated with colored lights. Then, having put the Hartford elite off its guard, he ushered them upstairs to preview *Modern French Paintings*, an exhibition of works by artists never before shown in Hartford—Cézanne, Van Gogh, Gauguin, Derain, Braque and Picasso.

That same year, Chick founded a musical subscription society he called with coy inclusiveness "The Friends and Enemies of Modern Music." (His letters to members always began, "Dear Friend or Enemy.") Between 1928 and 1942 the

FACING PAGE

TOP LEFT Salon, Chick Austin's
apartment, Hartford, 1928.

BOTTOM LEFT Entry hall, Chick
Austin's apartment, Hartford,
1928.

TOP RIGHT Sun porch, Chick
Austin's apartment, Hartford,
1928.

THIS PAGE
Courtship letters, Chick
Austin to Helen Goodwin,
on stationery with the
Morrison family crest, 1929.

Friends and Enemies presented premieres and early performances of works by composers as diverse as Igor Stravinksy, Ernst Krenek, Aaron Copland and Virgil Thomson. Austin told Hartford audiences to listen to the music of their own time, as he had done by attending many performances of the Ballets Russes, so that he "at least did not feel like one of the three little pigs in the presence of the big bad wolf."[18] The first concert was given at the Scarborough Street home of the museum's president, Charles Goodwin, on December 12, 1928. It was a daring two-piano performance by Harvard undergraduate and future composer Elliott Carter and his teacher, which began with Stravinsky's *Sacre du printemps,* followed by works of Milhaud, Schoenberg, Poulenc, Ives, Antheil, Satie and Hindemith.

It was characteristic of Austin's showmanship that only hours before the concert, he opened an exhibition of modern design in one of his two connecting apartments in Hartford. Inspired by the Paris exhibition three years earlier, he presented Art Deco furniture and decoration that he had bought and borrowed from firms like Lord & Taylor. Visitors walked through the first apartment with eighteenth-century French and Venetian furniture and into spaces where they gaped at such sights as a salon with black wall-to-wall carpeting under a silver ceiling with hand-blocked French wallpaper in black, white and gray, depicting little plump naked women among exotic birds and foliage, and a couch by Emile-Jacques Ruhlman in taupe velour, accented with triangular cushions of ivory and hyacinth blue. There was a hall decorated with citron, green and lemon wallpaper against lime-green woodwork and a sun porch with an eggplant carpet, coral drapes, walls of a blond wood veneer, a plush chair in turquoise and silver, a sofa bed in violet and rose, and a skyscraper bookstand painted black and Chinese red. The *Hartford Times* reporter was ecstatic about this museum director who had brought such a bold manifestation of the modern to town: "You will marvel at the ability of this young man, who is an artist in his own right."[19]

The only person who loaned a work of art to Chick's apartment exhibition—a watercolor of an artichoke in a wine glass by Yasuo Kuniyoshi—was Helen Goodwin. Her family had come to Hartford in the early seventeenth century. She was the daughter of the late Dean of Hartford's Christ Church Cathedral, the Reverend James Goodwin and his wife Frances Brown Goodwin, once known as one of the four "Hartford Belles." Helen was also the niece of the museum's president. She had taken every art course at Miss Porter's School, had studied at the Art Students League in New York and at art academies in Paris, and like Chick loved the Ballets Russes. Under her quiet, refined exterior, she was adventuresome enough to

27

have flown from London to Paris in 1927. She also had a sense of humor and a gift for mimicry. To their friends, Chick and Helen seemed like sides of the same rare coin. They called each other "Cunning," a term usually applied to adorable puppies or babies, for the rest of their lives. Although up to then Chick had been attracted mainly to the artistic young men he had met at Harvard, he fell deeply in love with Helen and could not get enough of her company. When he proposed marriage, she hesitated at the idea of marrying a whirlwind, but only briefly.

They were married in Paris on July 11, 1929, in the fashionable American Cathedral of the Holy Trinity, the Episcopal church on the Avenue George V

ABOVE Wedding album, Helen Goodwin Austin and Chick Austin, Paris, July 11, 1929.

RIGHT Villa Ferretti, Dolo, Italy, photograph by Chick Austin, 1929.

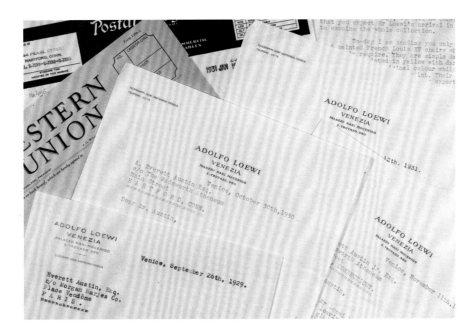

whore the Goodwins and their Morgan cousins of international banking fame, worshipped when they were in the French capital. Helen and Chick spent two months touring Europe, and while passing through the town of Dolo, near Venice on the Brenta River, they saw Scamozzi's Villa Ferretti of 1596. Its simple, clean lines appealed to them as the perfect style for the house they were planning to build on Goodwin land back in Hartford. They took snapshots of the villa to give to an architect after their return. In Venice they purchased fabrics, decorative objects and eighteenth-century architectural pieces from one of Chick's favorite antique dealers, Adolf Loewi. These included the Italian tempera panels and French mantel, the boiserie, and the antique blue-green silk brocatelle they would install in their living room and dining room. By the spring of 1930, their total acquisitions from Loewi amounted to $15,680.[20] This alone was about the same price as the land for the house, and many times Chick's salary, but he counted on his mother to pay the bills—sent to his office with increasing urgency—which she reluctantly did in installments until 1933.

Helen and Chick hired architect Leigh H. French, Jr., of New York, a friend of Helen's cousin, Philip Goodwin, who was later the architect with Edward Durrell Stone of the Museum of Modern Art. French specialized in American copies of French country houses of the *ancien regime*. He designed the house in close consultation with Helen and Chick, and work began in January 1930. As early as

ABOVE LEFT Bills to Chick Austin from Adolf (Adolfo) Loewi, 1929–1931.

ABOVE Helen Austin's household account book, showing Chick Austin's monthly allowance of $100 and lecture course income of $37.50, July 1934.

Austin House under construction, March 1930.

Austin House by Carl Van Vechten, c. 1931.

Austin House, rear exterior, c. 1935.

March, the *Hartford Times* published a prominent article about the "unusual house" that would soon appear on Scarborough Street, reproducing Leigh French's front elevation, a plan of the first floor and photographs of the interior decorative components.[21]

But Chick's desire to be part of every detail led French to withdraw in all but name. Henry-Russell Hitchcock watched the house develop, and later noted that French "was the first to say that the house was largely of Chick's design and hardly at all of his."[22] He also remembered that "the relief of the pilasters that line the front" was "carefully studied to give the proper effect at American scale and under American light conditions."[23] But later Chick decided that the architectural details, particularly the pilasters, were not standing out enough—not making enough of a statement, he said—and so the flat surfaces were painted a warm gray, while the doors and trim remained white, which made the house look even more like a theatrical flat than it had originally.

Austin's Atheneum programs early in 1930 reflected his artistic preoccupations. In January he presented America's first comprehensive Italian Baroque paintings exhibition, *Italian Painting of the Seventeenth and Eighteenth Centuries*, (essentially a translation of the title of the great Florence show), which was enhanced with French and Italian furniture and architectural elements from the period. Using his favorite metaphor, Chick later commented on the denigration of the baroque by some art critics: "Theatrical it may be, for the first great rise of the theater coincides with its development, and it may be truly said that the seventeenth century conceived of even the Church's ritual as dramatic spectacles for all the senses. The world itself had become a vast and exciting stage."[24]

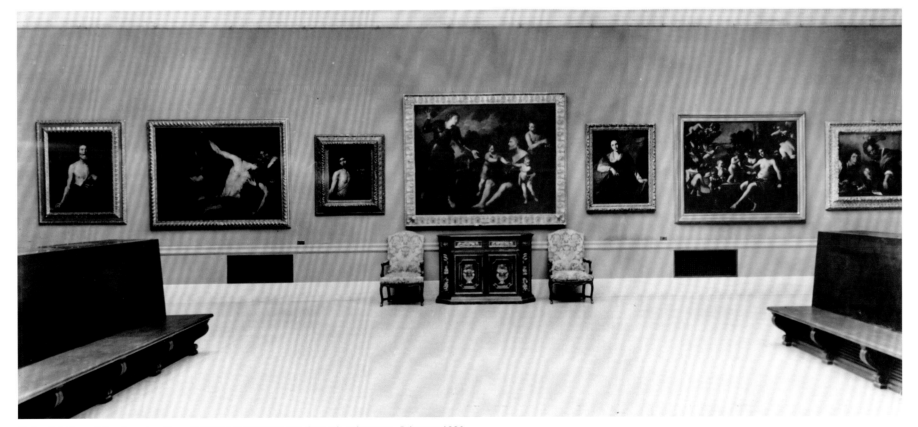

Italian Painting of the Seventeenth and Eighteenth Centuries, Wadsworth Atheneum, February 1930.

Chick Austin's office, Morgan Memorial, Wadsworth Atheneum,
Wassily chair and glass-topped table by Marcel Breuer, 1930.

Shortly after the show, Chick bought Bernardo Strozzi's *Saint Catherine of Alexandria*, an early seventeenth-century masterpiece, which he had seen in Florence in 1922. It was soon regarded as one of the finest Italian baroque pictures in the United States.

The Hartford show had an immediate impact on American museums. Collectors, dealers and educators responded to the attractions of the baroque. Austin's friend Agnes Mongan, a preeminent expert on old master drawings and director of the Fogg Art Museum, later declared: "It was Chick who started a whole American generation looking at Guercino, Feti, Strozzi—all those people who had never even been regarded before—and he bought *brilliantly*!"[25] The next edition of the standard college art history survey text, *Art Through the Ages*, by Helen Gardner, would include a new chapter: "Baroque Art in Italy in the Seventeenth Century."

Then in March, just as Chick was planning the modern rooms on Scarborough Street, he redecorated his office at the museum and opened it to the public as an exhibition of Bauhaus design, with a German tubular lighting fixture, walls of different shades of red and a tubular chair and table by Marcel Breuer. The line

between Austin's private and public life was always indistinct, and his office and his house were extensions of his activities at the museum.

He conferred regularly with Philip Goodwin about details of the house that spring and summer. "I still fear for the hall," he confessed, "but I think if we can get the right color on it, it will be all right."[26] In June he asked for the profile of the moulding Goodwin used for a hall in his own house in Syosset, New York, "which,

Helen Austin photographed in the rear hall of the Austin house, from the dining room,
The Hartford Times, May 7, 1938.

Chick Austin with David, 1933.

Helen Austin with David and Sally, 1936.

as I recall, had such a pleasant robust quality."[27] In July, with the house construction nearly complete, Austin told Goodwin: "It has innumerable faults, but nevertheless, I think it has been an amusing experiment and one from which I, at least, have learned a great deal."[28] The certificate of occupancy was issued on August 16. The Allyn Wadhams Company, the Hartford contractors, officially listed the construction cost at $43,000, $12,000 over the estimate. The entire cost of the house can be conservatively estimated at $80,000, a very high expenditure in 1930, for a relatively small house.[29] Chick's mother did pay the bills for most of the out of pocket expenditures, but the house also carried a mortgage in Helen Austin's name, as was customary to assure widows of tangible assets.

The grand opening of the house in December for Atheneum members was only the first of many events there over the next dozen years, and Chick and Helen continued to give tours—to his students at Trinity College, to his adult education classes at the museum, and to members of the public for the benefit of such institutions as the Hartford Art School. They provided visitors with a typed list of the furniture,

decorative objects and paintings in each room. A woman on one tour noticed an abstract oil on the wall and asked. "Is that a Picasso?" Chick replied with a smile: "I'm afraid it's only an Austin." One winter afternoon a group of schoolteachers who had taken a night course with him came to tea. As a large woman eased herself into a gilded chair in the living room in front of a blazing fire, it broke into pieces under her. Helping the mortified guest up, Chick said blithely: "Think nothing of it. These eighteenth-century chairs make the best firewood." And he threw the pieces into the fireplace.[30]

Just a year after the baroque show, Chick produced the first surrealist exhibition in any museum, in which Salvador Dali's freshly painted *Persistence of Memory* made its debut in the United States. His purchase of Dali's *Solitude* from the exhibition (for $150), the first such acquisition by a museum, opened the way for his other early acquisitions of important works by contemporary artists.

In 1933 Chick entered a new phase of life in two very different arenas. In January he and Helen had a baby boy, David Etnier Austin. The proud father added

Austin House, rear exterior with addition by architect
H. Sage Goodwin, Helen's cousin, c. 1940.

national Style. A sleek white court rose three stories to a skylight with long can-tilevered balconies, and in the center of the court amid all the floating planes, Austin daringly placed an Italian Mannerist marble sculpture of Venus with a nymph and satyr by Pietro Francavilla, dated 1600, in a shallow pool. Under the court was a tiny elegant theater that he designed in the Art Deco style. His office off the court, often open to the public for small exhibitions in the coming years, with its two Brazil-ian rosewood walls, white rubber floor, a desk of one piece of canaletta wood, and

an electric train set to his acquisitions, and the house became more than an enter-tainment venue. Two years later, Sarah Goodwin Austin—Sally—was born. The chil-dren had a long-term Scottish nurse from Glasgow whom they called "Munga" because they could not pronounce "Martha," her real name. David remembered Munga as "a wonderful, kindly disciplinarian."[31] Along with Helen, she was a source of stability as a series of cooks came and went and Chick pursued his unending proj-ects and activities.

The children shared a room at first, but when David was seven, Helen and Chick added a room to the back of the second floor, built over the rear terrace. Sally remembered that in the morning with their father up and gone before anyone else and their mother "unapproachable" until after she had her coffee and breakfast in bed, they learned to be self-sufficient. "We just did it ourselves. David did it. His room was very cold, so he would get dressed in front of the heater in the bathroom between our rooms. He would whistle away, so happy, and say, 'Get up, Sally, get up!'"[32]

At the Atheneum in 1933, Chick was preoccupied with the construction of a new wing to the museum, the Avery Memorial. After a considerable struggle with the architects, he virtually designed the interior of the building himself in the Inter-

Avery Court, Wadsworth Atheneum, with *Venus with Satyr and Nymph* of 1600 by Pietro Francavilla, during the Picasso exhibition, February 1934.

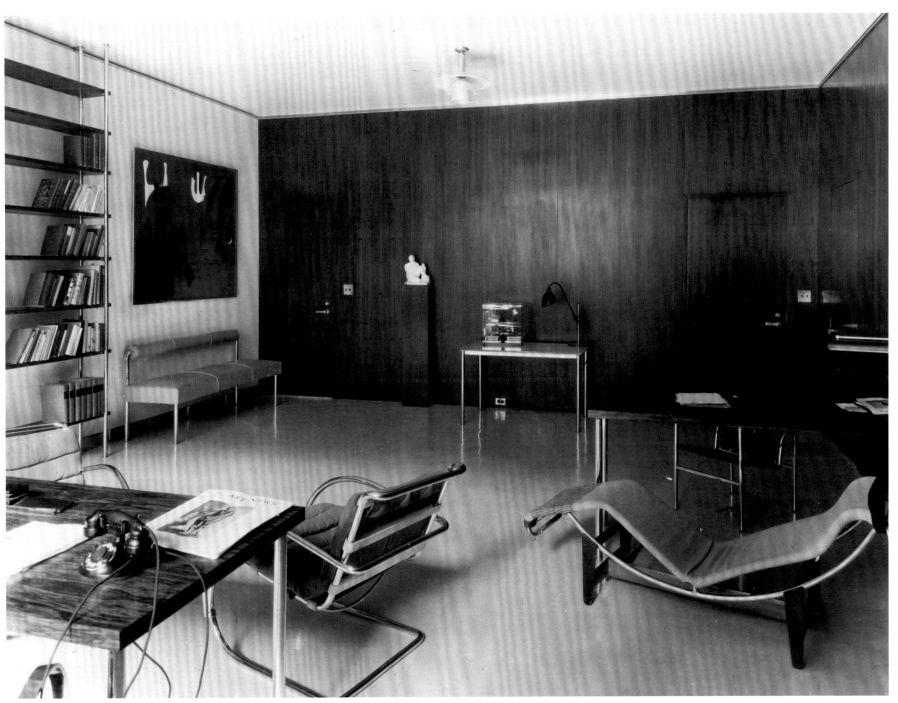

Chick Austin's office, Avery Memorial, Wadsworth Atheneum, showing the newly acquired Miró,
Composition, and furniture by Marcel Breuer and Le Corbusier, 1934. Only the telephone shows its age.

chromed tubular furniture by Breuer and Le Corbusier, was the ultimate in International Style elegance.

In July while planning the opening events for the building—America's first comprehensive Picasso show and the premiere of the opera *Four Saints in Three Acts* by Gertrude Stein and Virgil Thomson—Chick excitedly answered an urgent plea from his Harvard friend Lincoln Kirstein in London to sponsor choreographer George Balanchine's immigration to America to start a "School of American Ballet" and a dance company under the auspices of the Atheneum. Balanchine arrived in October, but he and Kirstein remained in Hartford only ten days before choosing New York as a more feasible location for their enterprise, to Chick's intense disappointment. By a happy coincidence, just a few weeks after their departure, Chick was able to make his single most important purchase of contemporary art, the incomparable Serge Lifar Collection of over 160 designs for the sets and costumes for Diaghilev's Ballets Russes. The drawings, watercolors and oils by artists such as Benois, Bakst, Matisse, Picasso, Braque, Derain, Léger, Miró, Gris, Modigliani, Rouault, Cocteau, de Chirico, Survage, Ernst, Bérard, Tcheltichew, Naum Gabo and Nathalie Goncherova, represented the celebrated ballets by such composers as Rimsky-Korsakov, Stravinsky, Ravel, Debussy, de Falla, Milhaud, Poulenc and Prokofiev—all for a bargain price of $10,000.

Austin's stunning acquisition was a worthy prelude to the grand opening, in early February 1934, of the Avery Memorial, the Picasso exhibition and *Four Saints in Three Acts*. The triple triumph elicited a cover article in *Art News* and stories in *Time* and *Newsweek*. Cultural commentator Henry McBride in the New York *Sun* quoted Picasso's dealer as saying: "At last there is one genuinely modern museum in the world."[33] The opera was a modernist epiphany with Gertrude Stein's amusingly cubist libretto ("Pigeons on the grass alas"), Virgil Thomson's surprisingly tuneful and touching score, painter Florine Stettheimer's sets of colored cellophane and costumes of lace, silks, satins, and gold and silver lamé, and an unprecedented all-black cast of singers from the Eva Jessye Choir and dancers choreographed by Frederick Ashton, making his American professional debut. The production was directed by John Houseman, his first work in the theater. The opera would go on to a record-breaking run on Broadway a few weeks later. Novelist and man-about-Harlem Carl Van Vechten wrote immediately to Gertrude Stein in Paris, comparing the opening of *Four Saints* favorably to that of Stravinsky's *Sacre du printemps*, which he had attended twenty-one years earlier.[34]

FACING PAGE Léon Bakst,
*Costume Design for Vaslav Nijinsky
as a Faun*, from the ballet,
Après-midi d'un faune, c. 1912.
Graphite, tempera and/or watercolor,
gold paint on illustration board, 15¹¹⁄₁₆
x 10¹¹⁄₁₆ inches, purchased 1935.

LEFT Picasso exhibition, Avery
Memorial, Wadsworth Atheneum,
February 1934.

BELOW *Four Saints in Three Acts*,
Avery Theater, Wadsworth
Atheneum, February 1934.

The all-night party at the Austin House after the opera was a delirious celebration. Guests included Mrs. John D. Rockefeller, Alfred Barr, Alexander Calder, Buckminster Fuller, Isamu Noguchi, Clare Boothe, Katherine Dreier, Virgil Thomson, Frederick Ashton, John Houseman, Julien Levy, and Florine Stetheimer. Years later both Calder and Levy, America's first major surrealist art dealer and a friend of Chick's from Harvard, published their versions of an incident at the party. Levy claimed that while congratulating Virgil Thomson, the composer self-consciously deflected him by pointing out that the trumpets had come in late in the second act, at which point Levy told him not to "split hairs" and teasingly pushed him. Thomson fell backward onto one of Chick's gold bamboo chairs, which broke into pieces. Calder, telling Levy that he was drunk, gently picked up the dealer and carried him to an upstairs bedroom. Levy acquiesced and waited for a few minutes before returning the party, recalling that each of them had been "overly considerate."[35] Calder, however, recorded that Levy was so intoxicated that he was blocking the staircase from the basement bar to the first floor and so he and James Thrall Soby, the collector and later curator of paintings at the Museum of Modern Art, removed him to the second floor. Calder wrote that when Levy reappeared he was

Chick Austin by Lee Miller, New York, December 1933.

anchine's *Transcendance* and *Alma Mater* and the American premiere of his *Mozartiana*.[37] For the first night, another glittering audience of out-of-town guests converged on Hartford, among them George Gershwin, the Salvador Dalis, newly arrived in America, the George Antheils, Sol Hurok, Sam Lewisohn, and Mrs. Nelson Rockefeller. Hartford's own Katharine Hepburn, a friend of the Austins, came to the final performance. The audience was wildly enthusiastic and calls for Balanchine did not let up until the diminutive choreographer came out on stage and made a shy bow. On Chick's thirty-fourth birthday a few days later, Dali spoke in the museum's theater in French, uttering for the first time his famous dictum: "The only difference between me and a madman is that I am not a madman."[38]

These were the heady days of what New Yorkers were calling "Chick's museum," when one memorable cultural figure followed another on the calendar. In January 1935, a month after Dali's appearance, Gertrude Stein spoke in the Avery theater on "Pictures and What They Are," telling the audience that "the relationship between the oil painting and the thing painted was really nobody's business."[39] The pronouncement elicited laughter, but it was in fact what every serious student of painting knew.

As Chick's reputation as an arbiter of taste, an impresario and a party-giver *par excellence* grew on both sides of the Atlantic, the Austins' guest list became increasingly international. In March Chick gave two Neo-Romantic artists their first solo museum exhibitions in America: Pavel Tchelitchew and Eugene Berman. Berman provided compelling testimony to the magnetism of Chick Austin and the experience of mounting a show with such a dynamo:

> No sooner had I landed in New York than I was whisked away on my first week end to see the Hartford museum and to meet the almost legendary man behind it: Chick Austin.
>
> This immediate visit to Hartford was not just an exceptional occurrence. It was a must with every newcomer to the American shores, with every new artist or leader in the plastic arts or music. . . . Hartford was then the big, new attraction, the museum to be seen and admired for a completely new style and approach to buying and displaying art.
>
> . . . At the end of an exhausting day of work, Chick would whisk us back home, cook a fabulous dinner, play records and often take us back to the museum cellar for a night stretch of more hard work. I have never encountered similar high spirits or endurance—he never seemed to tire or need any rest.[40]

When Berman saw Chick's house, he instantly recognized that its model was the Villa Ferretti, which he had sketched in 1931. He gave Chick the drawing in gratitude for the exhibition. Berman remembered, from many later visits, Chick's talent for design and his love of making new acquisitions:

"very indignant that we should have called attention to his inebriety, and remained in that state of indignation for about twenty years."[36]

Chick was, for the moment, the most famous museum director in the country, and true to form he plunged into significant new programs for the rest of 1934. Among them were a ten-week motion picture retrospective, the first of its kind in an American museum; a comprehensive exhibition of Man Ray's photographs; and for three days in December, after making peace with Lincoln Kirstein, the first public performances of the producing company of the School of American Ballet—the original ancestor of the New York City Ballet. This included the premieres of Bal-

A party in the "Blue Lagoon."
c. 1935. Helen and Chick
(both with cigarettes) flank
Helen's mother, Frances Goodwin
(seated), in the Austin House
dining room.

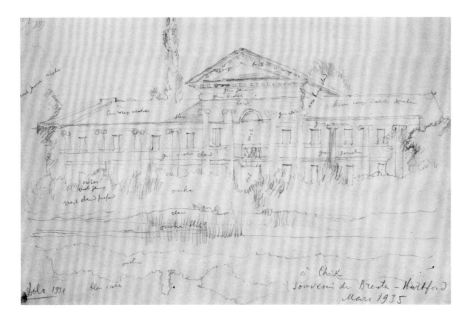

TOP Eugene Berman, *A Villa near Mira [Villa Ferretti]*, 1931.
Graphite on paper, 13¾ x 18⅛ inches, gift of David E. Austin, 1988.

BOTTOM *Abstract Art*, Avery Court, Wadsworth Atheneum, 1935.

And all that wonderful Italian Baroque and Rococo furniture and stuffs inside the house, all the *objects d'art* which Chick would collect for the house and continue to buy for other houses in other parts of the country with an unerring eye for unique quality in design, invention and exquisite workmanship. . . . Every new visit to Chick's, whether in his museum or to any of his houses, was to every one of his friends a source of supreme pleasure and discovery.[41]

Later in 1935 Le Corbusier spoke at the Atheneum on his first trip to America about the cities of the future with elevated expressways and tall buildings on stilts that looked like honeycombed glass boxes. When he returned to France and wrote about the trip in his book *When the Cathedrals Were White*, he declared:

This Hartford museum, with its youthful architecture, its joyous enlightenment, is only valuable because its director, Mr. Austin, and his two great friends, Messrs. [James Thrall] Soby and [Henry-Russell] Hitchcock, have a lively and optimistic spirit…. Thus Hartford, a small city far up in Connecticut, has become a spiritual center of America, a place where the lamp of the spirit burns."[42]

Le Corbusier's visit coincided with Chick's *Abstract Art* exhibition, which included sculptures and paintings by Piet Mondrian, Cesar Domela and Naum Gabo and his brother Antoine Pevsner. Chick placed their works in Avery Court with infinite care, and the show was stunningly futuristic. Chick called the exhibition "one of the most beautiful installations yet achieved by the museum."[43]

During this period, Chick and Helen occasionally hosted concerts for the Friends and Enemies of Modern Music at home. The most notable of these occurred on June 2, 1935. Hearing Virgil Thomson lament that wealthy patrons invited musicians to parties and then expected them to perform without charging a fee, Austin promptly invited four composers to play at his house with compensation under the auspices of the Friends and Enemies. As Thomson recorded in his memoirs, "Aaron Copland played pieces of mine and also his Piano Variations. I played portraits of a half-dozen people present and sang songs by Paul Bowles (one made from a letter of Gertrude Stein) and by Antheil (out of *Alice in Wonderland*). George Antheil played duets with me and by himself a Suite. Bowles offered portraits of the three other composers plus a Piano Sonatina."[44] Chick's gatherings almost always combined artistic talent with high hilarity and Bowles remembered the aftermath of the concert: "The occasion had its contretemps for me: somehow in the general drunkenness that followed the breakup of the evening, my suitcase disappeared. I could not very well go back to New York in white tie and tails; Austin had to lend me suit, shirt, tie, and socks in order for me to get out of Hartford."[45]

The young modernists—patrons, artists, performers, curators, scholars and art dealers—played as hard as they worked, but the gatherings at the Austins' house

THE FRIENDS AND ENEMIES OF MODERN MUSIC, INC

SEVENTH SEASON 1934-1935

May 2, 1935

Dear Friend or Enemy:

The Friends and Enemies of Modern Music, Inc., wish to announce
the third event of their 1934-1935 season, which will be held at the
home of Mr. and Mrs. A. Everett Austin, Jr., 130 Scarborough Street,
Hartford, on Monday evening, May thirteenth, at eight-thirty o'clock.

An evening of unusual interest has been planned for this occasion. Four well-known American composers, George Antheil, Aaron
Copland, Paul Bowles, and Virgil Thomson, will make comments and
play informally some of their own works.

It is sincerely hoped that all members will attend. So that
we may make the necessary arrangements, will you be good enough to
let us know how many seats you would like reserved? A limited number of guest tickets will be available at $2.00 each. Kindly com-
municate with Miss Eleanor Howland, Avery Memorial, Hartford, -
telephone 7-6421.

Very sincerely yours,

A. Everett Austin, Jr.
President

A. EVERETT AUSTIN, Jr., President   Mrs. A. EVERETT AUSTIN, Jr., Treasurer   Mrs. BARCLAY ROBINSON, Secretary

LEFT Chick Austin to the Friends and Enemies of Modern Music, May 3, 1935. Although scheduled for May 13, the concert at the Austin House was postponed to June 2.

ABOVE A gathering in Chick Austin's office, Avery Memorial, Wadsworth Atheneum, January 21, 1936. Austin and guests look at Eugene Berman's design sketches for the upcoming Hartford Festival. Left to right: Chick Austin, James Thrall Soby, Mimi Soby, Henry Kneeland, Beatrice Kneeland, Eleanor Howland, Eugene Berman, Henry-Russell Hitchcock, Helen Austin, Paul Cooley and Mrs. Edward Stimson.

offered them innumerable opportunities for creative synergy as they exchanged news and ideas and planned collaborations.

Chick's most ambitious entertainment came in February 1936, when the Friends and Enemies produced a week of musical events—the Hartford Festival. In addition to a film series, there was an evening of music and dance. Russian singers from New York performed Stravinsky's dramatically percussive *Les Noces*. Next came the American premiere of Erik Satie's symphonic drama, *Socrate*, with

a huge mobile set by Alexander Calder, consisting of red, black and white discs. The program ended with a specially commissioned ballet by Balanchine, *Serenata*, with music by Mozart and décor by Pavel Tchelitchew, in which dancers appeared with lighted candles on their heads and the great ballerina from the Ballets Russes, Felia Doubrovska, danced publicly for the last time.

It all culminated in the Paper Ball, "Le Cirque des Chiffoniers," for which Chick commissioned Tchelitchew to transform Avery Court into a fantasy of painted

41

Avery Court decorated by Pavel Tchelitchew for the Paper Ball of February 15, 1936.

newspapers that covered the cantilevered balconies and the skylight. Chick also asked Tchelitchew, Calder and other artists to design costumes for the ball. In his case, Chick was a Ringmaster in a red top hat and a red paper jacket, waving a whip. Helen was dressed by Tcheltichew in a flowery creation as "Summer." Balanchine and Lincoln Kirstein were disguised as exotic beggars, and Hitchcock wore brown paper cut in the shape of an elephant by Calder over a costume by Tcheltichew called "Architecture." From New York came actress Ruth Ford, who appeared as the "Muse of Poetry" in a cellophane dress by Tchelitchew, singing a new song by Vernon Duke and carried on a litter by her brother Charles Henri Ford, Parker Tyler and other handsome young men, dressed as cowboys and Indians—all of them wearing makeup and false eyelashes, to the horror of "Old Hartford." The New York press raved about the beauty and invention of the Paper Ball, but it lost about a thousand dollars, and the trustees began to tire of Chick's entertainments. Their disapproval slowed Austin only slightly.

In January 1938, he brought Lincoln Kirstein's Ballet Caravan, a company drawn from the School of American Ballet, to Hartford. The program included the premiere of the first quintessentially American ballet, *Filling Station*, with music by Virgil Thomson, choreography by Lew Christiansen, who also danced the lead, and décor by the painter Paul Cadmus. These performances coincided with the unveiling of fanciful murals on the theater's walls, which Chick had commissioned from Kristians Tonny, the Dutch Neo-Romantic painter. Once again, there was a tremendous party at the Austins' house for the musicians, artists, dancers, and Austin's friends. The aftermath of the celebration left some of the participants at bit disoriented. Paul Cadmus recalled that in the middle of the night Kirstein was temporarily under the impression that he had turned into an alligator.[46]

Later in the year Chick and Helen entertained the entire company of the Ballet Russe de Monte Carlo at their house after a performance in Hartford's Bushnell Auditorium. Chick whipped up a sumptuous meal for the dancers, ravenous after their exertions (his specialties ranged from chicken provençale

Avery Theater after the installation of the murals by Kristians Tonny, 1938.

to eggplant dishes and airy soufflets), and as usual played records of everything from Gershwin and Cole Porter to modern French, German and Russian composers far into the night. What the trustees thought of these non-stop parties is not documented, but they were increasingly skeptical about the out-of-town Bohemians being entertained at all hours. Reserved as Helen seemed on the surface, she thrived on the excitement Chick created in Hartford. That same year, during a lull, she wrote to Tonny's wife Marie-Claire after the couple had returned to Europe, letting them know how much she missed the stimulation of their presence in Hartford: "There is really very little to tell you, as you know how dull it is here, and it is really worse than when you were here, though you won't believe it!"[47]

By the end of the 1930s, David and Sally Austin were old enough to enjoy their father's playful spontaneity and the characters he invited to the house. They remembered seeing Chick randomly setting off firecrackers by the river in back of the house, Calder dancing on a table like a bear, and the famous magician Harry Blackstone (with bodyguard in tow) making the hors d'oeuvres in the living room disappear.[48]

The children shared their father's love of animals, but came to recognize their mother's difficulty with Chick's changing menagerie. In 1932, to support the Children's Art Classes that he had initiated at the museum, Chick resumed his childhood magic shows, calling himself "The Great Osram" after the German company that produced the light bulbs in Helen's dressing room. Each year they became more elaborate. Before one show Helen noticed a gamey aroma arising from the radiator grates on the first floor. She investigated and found the laundry room filled with rab-

bits for the magic tricks running free. They were banished to a studio Chick rented in downtown Hartford, where he designed sets and costumes for his theatrical activities. When David was born, Chick bought a dachshund puppy for his son. Knowing that Helen did not like dogs, he kept the puppy in a bureau drawer for a week while he thought about how to convince his wife that this would be a good thing. Helen was not pleased with the surprise, but eventually became attached to Elsa, as she was called. Elsa had many successors in the family, including another dachshund, Bobby, and a black Labrador retriever named Nera. Helen's biggest animal surprise came when Chick arrived home from visiting his mother in New Hampshire,

Members of the company of the Ballet Russe de Monte Carlo are entertained at the Austin House after a performance at Hartford's Bushnell Auditorium, November 29, 1938.

Helen Austin with David and Sally in the Austin House living room, c. 1938.

carrying a mangy monkey somehow acquired from a woman he had met when stopping for gas in Worcester. As Sally recalled, "Ma really hit the roof. She made him take it to the SPCA, and the lady who got it from them cured it of mange, and it became the great person in her life. She sent us Christmas cards for years thanking us and reporting, 'My monkey's doing so well.'"[49]

The children were also entranced by Chick's cars. It was said that he acquired them as often as he changed his wrist-watches—and he would frequently surprise Helen and the children with what he drove home from his travels. Early on, he had an English Sunbeam with the words "Wadsworth Atheneum" emblazoned on the side of its hood. Later there was an English Sparrow, a Lancia, a Porsche, a Jaguar, a gull-wing Mercedes, a Bentley, and finally a Rolls-Royce.

But for all the amusement and glamour, most of what Austin did was hard work. Considering that the entire professional staff of the museum consisted of about five people, their productivity was enormous. Born teacher that he was, Austin was a pioneer in producing theme shows, and throughout his tenure he explored genres of painting, all of them spanning centuries, all of them combining the Atheneum's collection with loans of equally high quality—landscapes, portraits, and, in 1938, the first major still life exhibition in America. In 1940, with the coming of the Second World War in Europe, he presented *Night Scenes*. Three years later, as the United States became fully engaged in the war, he offered *Men in Arms*, destined to be his last show. The destruction in Europe and the threat to America appalled Austin, who expressed his anxiety in a plea for greater support of the museum's programs in his 1941 annual report to the trustees: "The record of the great culture of Western civilization must not be imperiled. . . . Beauty is not a luxury. . . . It will not really be the guns and ships, important as they are, that will eventually conquer, but the spirit which animates them."[50]

In 1941 he branched out and starred in his own production of *Hamlet*. He looked the part, but there was concern from his trustees about the director appearing in tights in the museum. And all the modern art business seemed to be getting out hand with purchases of pictures by Dali, Klee, Arp and Max Ernst,

The Great Osram as "The Sea-God of Magic" in his final magic show as director, Avery Theater, December 1944. Chick Austin designed the set and costume.

Chick Austin in his studio designing a set for the Little Theater of Hartford, 1940.

Helen Austin with Elsa, Windham, New Hampshire, c. 1935.

Sally Austin poses as a *Vogue* model with her new Mercedes in front of the Austin House, c. 1957.

Chick Austin as Hamlet, 1941.

whose painting *Europe After the Rain*, a harbinger of the Holocaust and Hiroshima, Chick bought in 1942.

By the spring of 1943, with much of the collection in storage to protect it from bombing and his art history courses at Trinity cancelled for the duration, Chick became restless and provocative. He presented John Ford's early sixteenth-century Jacobean play, whose famous title, *'Tis Pity She's a Whore*, was shortened politely to *'Tis Pity*. Chick played the protagonist, who impregnates his sister and murders her to save her from shame. The play was a manifestation of the baroque comparable to some of the Italian pictures of the period, but his audience found it distasteful in the extreme, and there were outraged letters to the local papers.

Depressed and longing to escape, Chick requested a six-month leave of absence, which was granted. He went alone to Hollywood to recuperate, with an invitation from a dealer friend to stay at the Garden of Allah, the former residence of actress Alla Nazimova that was something between a private club and a luxury hotel with bungalows around a pool. The trustees back in Hartford considered it an extraordinary address. Just before he drove to California at the beginning of July, he made his last major purchase for the Atheneum, *The Ecstasy of Saint Francis* by Caravaggio, the first genuine work by the seminal Italian baroque painter in an American museum. He also threw one more party at the house, which was filled with his local admirers and hangers-on—magic assistants, stage hands, Trinity students, dancers, musicians and actors. As he wrote to his friend Truda Kaschmann, a gifted teacher of modern dance from Germany, who was in attendance, "I am told our final scene was played not without a certain tenderness. It must have been the Pernod. It always gives me an attack of combined amnesia and lethargy."[51]

Chick loved the Los Angeles of those days and became a friend of Angela Lansbury, her mother the British actress Moyna Macgill and her brothers Edgar and Bruce. He also got to know Igor and Vera Stravinsky, Vincent Price, Joan Fontaine, and fellow New Englander Bette Davis. For a house he acquired in the Hollywood hills, he bought eighteenth-century furnishings from his old friend from Venice, Adolf Loewi, who had moved his family to Los Angeles just before the War. With Edgar Bergen, Walter Huston, Charles Coburn, and others, Chick founded the Gate Studio Theater. Hartford seemed far away, and by December he had obtained an extension of his leave from the trustees.

Helen accepted Chick's need to find his equilibrium. Meanwhile she had turned the front lawn on Scarborough Street into a Victory Garden and had closed the south side of the first floor of the house, moving the piano and some of the living room furniture into the dining room to save on the increasing cost of fuel oil.

During Chick's absence the trustees discovered paintings valued at about $60,000 in the basement, sent on approval by dealers, which he had not brought to the attention of the board. They dispatched the list to Chick and told him sternly to choose several of them as a good will gesture. Chick called the business a tempest in a teapot because the dealers were all his friends. But he chose several works for the Atheneum, including Gauguin's mysterious *Nirvana*, a portrait of the artist's friend Meyer de Haan.

When he returned to Hartford in the spring of 1944, the board told him that unless he agreed to produce more popular exhibitions and show more appreciation for Hartford's sensibilities, he could not stay. Chick reminded them of what he had done for the museum and made it clear that he would not compromise his artistic standards. It was announced that A. Everett Austin, Jr., would be leaving the Wadsworth Atheneum after seventeen years, as of January 1, 1945. He was forty three. Alfred Barr, the founding director of the Museum of Modern Art, when he heard the news, wrote to Chick in disbelief: "But you did things soon and more brilliantly than anyone. You made us gay—and envious and no one can replace you."[52]

Three months later his mother died, leaving Chick a trust fund (with the principal to go to his children at his death), but her estate was not fully settled for well over a year. Helen and Chick decided to lease the Hartford home to cousins and move for a year to Chick's house in Hollywood.

At the beginning of 1946, just as Chick found himself at the lowest point of his career, the governor of Florida asked Edward Forbes to recommend a man to be the first director of the John and Mable Ringling Museum of Art, the pink and white palace on Sarasota Bay that held the largest collection of baroque and rococo paintings in America. As he had in 1927, Forbes suggested Chick Austin, who was immediately offered the job. Situated on more than sixty acres, the museum included the Circus King's spectacular mansion, Cà d'Zan, modeled on the Doge's Palace in Venice, with a splendid reception room for concerts and dramatic readings. Before taking up his position at the Ringling, Chick started a summer theater, the Windham Playhouse, in a barn on his mother's estate, a popular enterprise he continued until his death.

While Helen, David and Sally remained in Los Angeles, Chick started work in Florida in October, though he visited as often as he could. The children remembered seeing Moyna Macgill nearly every Sunday afternoon and regarded the Lansburys as their second family while they were in California.[53] They did not return to the Hartford house until 1948.

Helen Austin with Sally and David at home in Hollywood, 1947.

In Sarasota Chick began plans to conserve the museum's collection, which had been seriously neglected during ten years of litigation after Ringling's death. He soon opened both the museum and the mansion to the public and initiated a series of loan exhibitions, musical programs, an annual seminar featuring his distinguished friends in the art world, children's art classes, and a regular film series. He also made the first new acquisitions since John Ringling, beginning with a superb portrait by Rubens. In 1948 he started the Museum of the American Circus on the grounds of the museum with circus wagons, costumes and ephemera, the first serious museum of its kind in the United States, which grew to extraordinary proportions over the years.

In 1950 Chick purchased, from Adolf Loewi, the painted and gilded interior of the tiny jewel-like eighteenth-century theater from Asolo, Italy, and installed it in a large gallery in the museum. He opened it early in 1952 with two eighteenth-century operas, Pergolesi's *La Serva Padrona*, designed by Eugene Berman, and Mozart's *Bastien et Bastienne*, for which Chick designed the sets and costumes. The glamorous event brought an enthusiastic article by Virgil Thomson in the *New York Herald Tribune*, along with superlatives about "the genius of A. Everett Austin, Jr." in the Florida press.[54]

FAR LEFT Courtyard and loggia at the John and Mable Ringling Museum of Art, Sarasota, Florida, c. 1957.

LEFT Chick Austin at the Ringling Museum, 1947.

BELOW Cà d'Zan, the Ringling winter residence.

Meanwhile, in 1947, he had bought a large 1920s Spanish-style stucco house, which he named "Villa Cirque" (but referred to as "Termite Towers") in the Del Mar estates, near the museum, and decorated it with the eighteenth-century fabrics, furniture and objects that he collected. By 1950 his summer theater was making a handsome profit, which Austin admitted to friends, as he headed for Europe, would quickly disappear: "I was cooking for seven as well as acting and doing everything else but I have fifteen hundred smackers in my jeans for my trouble and it wont take a moment to exchange it for some 18th century fripperies I suppose."[55]

Throughout this period, Chick had developed a yearly pattern of arriving in Sarasota in October, returning to Hartford on his birthday a week before Christmas, spending a few days in New York early in the new year before driving back to Florida, opening his major winter exhibition in February or March, for which Helen would come to stay for a few weeks, then going up to New Hampshire in June to open his theater, stopping at Hartford on the way. Helen would visit him in Windham, and he would see her in Castine, Maine, where the Goodwin family spent summers. In late August or early September, he would travel to Europe for a month or six weeks, return to Hartford and then drive to Sarasota to begin the year again. Living in his guest house in Sarasota was Chick's former Trinity student and magic assistant, Jim Hellyar, who gave him companionship, help with his museum projects, and perhaps most important of all, an audience, for Chick hated being alone. Helen and Chick were in touch continuously by correspondence and telephone. His long letters to "Dearest Cunning" leave no doubt that despite his peripatetic life, she remained not only his wife, but his closest friend and confidante as well.

Although Chick continued to find objects for his Sarasota home, he was always involved in decorative changes in Hartford. The most extensive redecorating came in 1950. The silk in the dining room had become so shabby that it needed replacement and he suggested a flowery eighteenth-century-style print with a light green background that he had found in Paris. He sent Helen samples for her approval and decorated his bedroom in Sarasota in the same fabric. While in Hartford that year, Chick also decided to marbleize the woodwork in the front hall to give the space a feeling of greater solidity. Assisted by his son David and Helen's niece Jane Goodwin, Chick did the work himself with a sponge, a brush and the ends of broken sticks. It was not finished by the time Chick had to return to Florida, so Helen hired a painter to finish the job, presumably the upper reaches of the molding around the dome.

More changes came after the flood of 1955 in Hartford. The Park River behind the house rose so high that the basement took in four feet of water, destroying the Chareau hanging bed and 78 rpm records of Chick's radio broadcasts. The moisture affected the first floor as well, and the walls in the living room were re-canvassed and repainted in a lighter green.

Chick Austin to Helen Austin, discussing the proposed new French fabric for the Austin House dining room, May 2, 1950.

SICILIAN CARVED, GILDED AND PAINTED LOUIS XV COMMODE circa 1740

Italian, 2nd quarter of the 18th century

H. 35"
L. 48"
D. 21"

Richly decorated with painted scenes of.ladies and cavaliers on two serpentine drawers, framed with gilded gesso scrollwork. At either end larger figures similarly framed. Cabriole legs with masquerone painted in grisaille. The conforming top of simulated reddish-brown marble.

Purchased from Ugo Ciardiello, Florence, 1950

Cost: NJJ

Meanwhile Chick was absorbed in another decorating adventure. A year earlier, as a base for his autumn travels on the Continent, he had bought a small seventeenth-century villa in the hill town of Fayence in Provence and began restoring and decorating it with objects he found among local dealers. He had fallen in love with the town two years earlier when he, Helen, and the children had traveled together for three weeks in a Citroën throughout Europe on their one extended family vacation.

By 1956, David had graduated from Harvard and was in the architecture school there, while Sally had attended art school in Florence after graduation from the Concord Academy. At the Ringling, Chick seemed as busy and creative as ever, planning a new building for the Asolo Theater. But in the fall of that year, when he arrived in France to pick up his new Rolls Royce Silver Cloud I in Cherbourg and drive it to Fayence, he seemed suddenly to have aged. He complained of severe back pain and when he came home to Scarborough Street on his fifty-sixth birthday in December, he was too ill to sleep upstairs. A bed was brought into the dining room for him and placed in the Bavarian alcove. He soon entered Hartford Hospital, with Helen in constant attendance, and was diagnosed with an inoperable tumor of the spine, which had spread from lung cancer. To the disbelief of his friends throughout the art world, he died in the hospital on March 29, 1957.

Beneath his theatrical flair and his love of entertainments, Austin was a serious museum professional whose pioneering museum work—his exhibitions, acquisitions and programs of live performances—rose to the highest level. The day after Austin died, the editor of *Art News*, Alfred Frankfurter, told a newspaper reporter: "I have known him for almost 30 years, and from the vantage point of editor of the oldest U.S. art magazine, which gives a unique opportunity for scanning the entire field. . . . A. Everett Austin was perhaps the most creative and original of art museum directors in the century since such institutions came into being."[56] Among the hundreds of tributes that were sent to Helen from many parts of the world was one from the scholar and connoisseur A. Hyatt Mayor, a longtime curator at the Metropolitan Museum of Art: "Chick's death deprives our generation of its finest mind. None of us had his prophetic flair, or his breadth of perception which made him the pilot intelligence of us all."[57] Helen, who had both loved and withstood a whirlwind, admitted to a friend that it had not been easy—"but he ennobled my life."[58]

Chick Austin's artistic interests were central to his life, and his museum activities were indivisible from the objects and spaces with which he lived. The Austin House embodies an unprecedented period of innovation when the arts seemed to be evolving every few months. As the British art historian and curator Stephen Calloway has pointed out, "art history in the twentieth century is not a single story about the rise and triumph of modernism," for the modernists themselves spearheaded the discovery and adaptation of past styles.[59] Chick was part of a daring group of young tastemakers on both sides of the Atlantic in the 1920s and '30s who loved the decadent drama and fantasy of the baroque-rococo as much as they loved being modern. Chick was not the only arbiter of the arts who felt free to combine elements of the past with the latest streamlined styles to create a new and more glamorous modernity. It could be found in the designs for Diaghilev's Ballets Russes, the fashion photography of Cecil Beaton, in Hollywood sets and the modern homes of sophisticated Europeans like the patron and collector Charles de Beistegui. His stark white Paris apartment was designed by Le Corbusier but turned into a baroque fantasy by architect Emilio Terry who designed neo-rococo chairs and commodes for it in white or blue and gold and installed sconces, gilded mirrors and Venetian chandeliers. The apartment was later embellished with a surreal roof garden inspired by Salvador Dali.[60] It is no coincidence that such an apartment—in what was still the artistic capital of the world—was built in 1930, the same year as the Austin house. Chick's "Pasteboard Palace" was a manifestation of the freshest aesthetic currents beyond the bounds of Hartford. Yet, in retrospect, its mere presence elevated the city to a higher sphere.

FACING PAGE A page from Chick Austin's record book of personal acquisitions, featuring a Sicilian carved, gilded and painted Louis XV commode, c. 1740. It was purchased in Florence in 1950 for his Sarasota bedroom and moved to the Austin House dining room by Helen Austin in 1957.

ABOVE RIGHT Chick and Helen Austin at Sally Austin's graduation from the Concord Academy, 1954.

RIGHT Chick Austin's bedroom, Sarasota, Florida, 1957. Helen Austin moved the eighteenth-century Dutch mirror to the front hall of the Austin House in 1957.

Austin House front hall, 1995.

Helen remained in the house the rest of her long life. Within a month of Chick's death, she and Sally went to Florida to settle Chick's affairs and sell the house. Before anything was touched, Helen had a professional photographer in Sarasota document the rooms just as they were when Chick left for Hartford the previous December. She chose her favorite eighteenth-century objects to add to the house on Scarborough Street—paintings, painted commodes and chairs, gilded mirrors, a Neapolitan settee from the living room, a Nymphenberg console table and chandelier from the dining room, and, from the entry hall, a white and gold console table from Würzburg, with two Mozartian soapstone sculptures and a covered Faience covered dish on top of it—which she placed in the entry hall in Hartford with a tall Dutch mirror from his bedroom over it. These objects fit easily into the spaces Chick had first designed. They were all his taste—and Helen's too. Other things were returned to dealers, particularly Adolf Loewi, for the prices Chick had paid. The Rolls, bought on credit, was sold through an advertisement in the *New York Times*.

Helen lived much as she always had, actively supporting the Atheneum, the Hartford Symphony, the Hartford Art School, Trinity College, the Episcopal Cathedral, and other institutions that she loved. She spent the summers in Castine, and made occasional trips to Europe. She and the Goodwin family were instrumental in the building of the Austin Arts Center of 1965 at Trinity and endowing the A. Everett Austin, Jr. Gallery in the Atheneum's new Goodwin Building of 1969 at the Atheneum. Occasionally, she entertained distinguished visitors to the Atheneum and Trinity College at the house.[61]

In 1981 the Atheneum turned its attention to its long neglected Archives, scattered in disarray in boxes, basements and closets throughout the museum's five connected buildings. Among them, in a sub-basement, were all of Chick Austin's papers—assumed by the outside world, including his family, to have been lost—covering his entire seventeen-year tenure as director, a cache amounting to more than 20,000 pages. This find, coupled with taped interviews of many of his friends conducted by the museum in the mid-1970s and supplemented with many additional interviews, led to a new appreciation of the achievements of the Austin era in Hartford and beyond.

In 1983 the museum invited Philip Johnson to share his memories of the opening of the Avery, the Picasso show, and *Four Saints in Three Acts* on the fiftieth anniversary of those events. There had been occasional mention of the preservation of the Austin house by Helen Austin, Hartford architect Jared Edwards, and Henry-Russell Hitchcock, who as America's most prominent architectural historian understood the unique position it occupied in the history of American culture. When asked for his opinion, Johnson remarked, "The house is much more important now than [Chick] ever could have known," adding that it should be given to the museum and made a National Historic Landmark.[62] When he spoke in the museum's theater in February 1984, he declared that Austin was "the center around which everything revolved," that his influence could not be exaggerated, and that at the opening of the Avery in 1934, the Wadsworth Atheneum was "at the center of the culture of the West." He spoke at length about the Austins' house, playfully suggesting that Chick had "some magical foretaste" of the future of architecture and design, even beyond the modernism of his time: "There it sits on Scarborough Street—a post-modern house, if you please, fifty years ago."[63] Soon afterward, their mutual friend Lincoln Kirstein echoed the sentiment. In its simplified Palladianism, the house was, he wrote, "the first example of Post-Modernism, *avant la lettre,*—in fact before 'modernism' had even triumphed."[64]

The Atheneum's board of trustees decided that the museum should preserve the Austin House by making it a permanent component of the museum itself. In March of 1984 the trustees invited Helen, David and Sally Austin to consider donating the Austin house and its contents to the Atheneum if new funding could be found to ensure that it would be restored and maintained in perpetuity. Helen's cousin, Mrs. James Lippincott Goodwin, enthusiastically agreed that should the Austin family accept the Atheneum's invitation, she would pay for the maintenance of the house and related curatorial salaries in her lifetime and bequeath more than sufficient funds to care for the house.

By February of 1985, Helen Austin had become too frail to remain at home and arrangements were made for her to move to a nearby nursing care facility. As she left the Scarborough Street house for the last time, taking only essentials with her, Helen, along with David and Sally, presented the Wadsworth Atheneum with the deed to their home of fifty-five years.

In November at the Atheneum's annual meeting, the board of trustees honored the Austin family with a resolution, declaring that the house, "a Hartford landmark since its construction in 1930, has been intimately linked with the Wadsworth Atheneum, its collections and its history," and thanking them for their "historic act of generosity."[65]

Among the first to congratulate the Atheneum on its foresight was the eminent architectural historian Colin Rowe of Cornell University. He suggested that the Austin House should "be interpreted as a theater of historical confrontations" and "an important *mise-en-scene* for the pol-

Charles de Beistegui's Paris apartment, designed by Le Corbusier and decorated by Emilio Terry, 1930.

TOP David and Sally Austin join their mother at the dinner in her honor at Trinity College on May 14, 1965. The Austin Arts Center at the college was dedicated the following day.

ABOVE David and Sally Austin and Philip Johnson with Genevieve Harlow Goodwin at the New York Academy of Art at the luncheon honoring her for endowing the Austin House, April 16, 1987.

itics of art in the 1930's. . . . It is quite as much one of the important monuments of Hartford as is the house of Mark Twain. . . . For the Wadsworth Atheneum to maintain and to preserve this house would be a major service to Hartford, to New England and to the nation."[66]

The board established a trustees committee to oversee and administer the house and develop plans for its restoration, preservation and use as an integral part of the Atheneum. They appointed a curator who began research on the history of the house, its collections, and the Austin family. An Austin House Advisory Board was created, including such friends of Chick Austin as Rosamond Bernier, Ruth Ford, Henry-Russell Hitchcock, John Houseman, Philip Johnson, Lincoln Kirstein, Angela Lansbury, Russell Lynes, Agnes Mongan, May Sarton, Virgil Thomson, Marguerite Yourcenar, and Edward M. M. Warburg.

Helen Austin died in July of 1986 at the age of eighty-eight. Her cousin Tulie Goodwin remained keenly interested in the plans for the Austin House and its eventual restoration until her own death three years later.

Research and exterior improvements to the house continued over the next few years. In 1994, the Secretary of the United States Department of the Interior designated the Austin House a National Historic Landmark, and in 1998 a meticulous interior restoration began in earnest, carried out according to *The Secretary of the Interior's Standards for the Treatment of Historic Properties*, and was essentially completed in 2007.

In the twenty-first century, visitors to the Austin House who pass through its streamlined Palladian façade enter the vibrant world that Chick Austin and an international cast of creative spirits brought to Hartford. For them, being modern included inventing, rediscovering, and presenting to as wide an audience as possible the artistic visions of many centuries, especially those of their contemporaries.

In 1936, knowing that what he was trying to accomplish at the Atheneum would not perhaps be fully understood until later, Austin expressed his mission as a museum director and an educator to a New York audience: "I have tried to make of the Avery Memorial in Hartford a museum of living things—pictures, sculpture, architecture, decorative arts, even movies and music—as well as of fine examples of the past. For we must have the great things of the past to enjoy and to study, but with that valuable experience and pleasure as guide and criterion, we must surely seek to live in the present and to try to create the new forms which are to be our legacy to the future."[67]

Chick Austin's legacy remains vividly alive in Hartford—in the architecture and the collections he created at the Wadsworth Atheneum and in the house on Scarborough Street, where the magic of his taste and imagination is palpable. It is a magic that still enchants, enlightens and inspires.

Avery Memorial, Wadsworth Atheneum, north entrance, 2004

Chick Austin by George Platt Lynes, 1936.

THE AUSTIN HOUSE
AFTER THE 1940 ADDITON

1 FRONT ENTRY HALL
2 PASSAGE
3 MUSIC ROOM
4 LIVING ROOM
5 REAR HALL
6 ELEVATOR
7 DINING ROOM
8 PANTRY
9 KITCHEN
10 PANTRY
11 REAR TERRACE

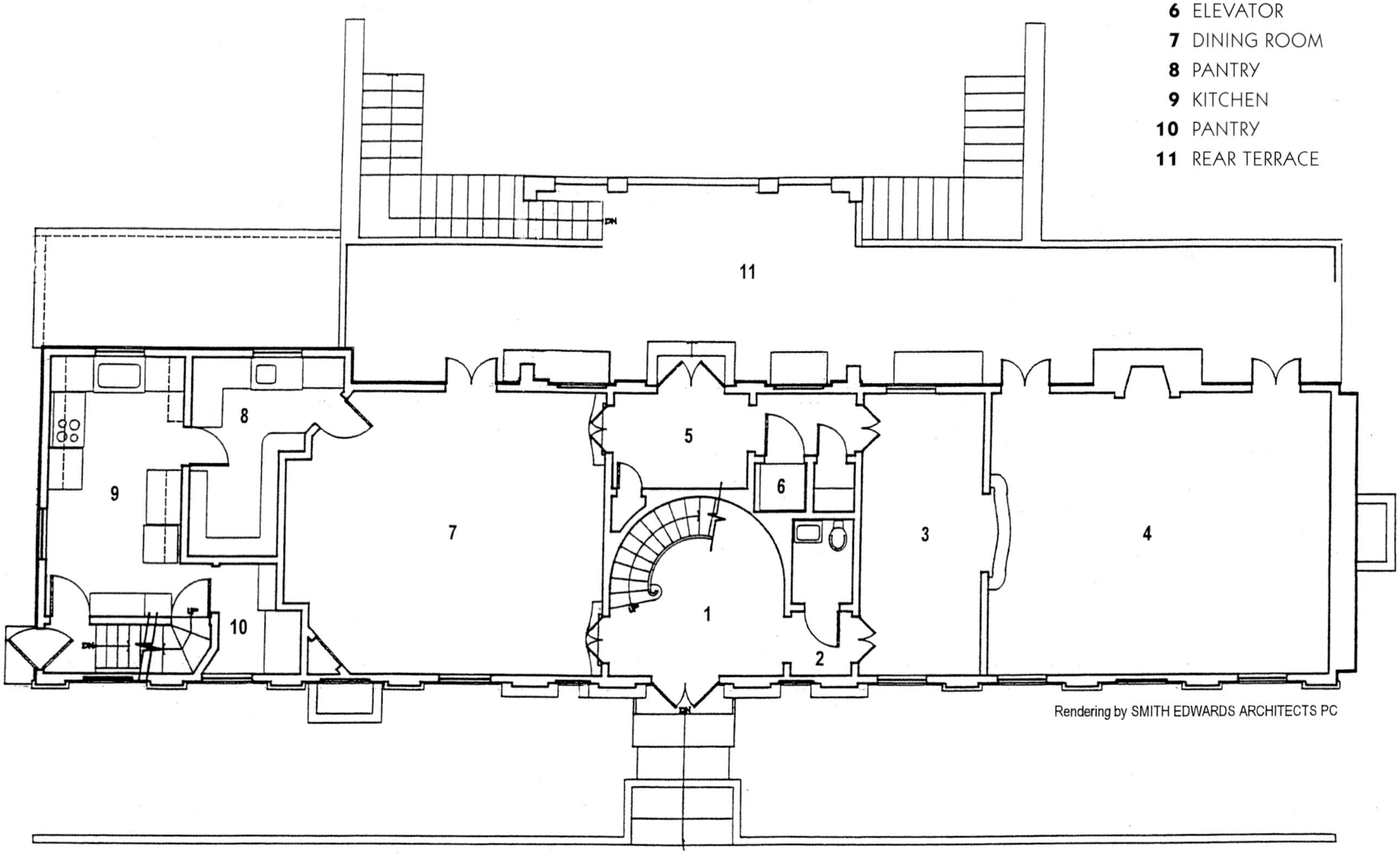

Rendering by SMITH EDWARDS ARCHITECTS PC

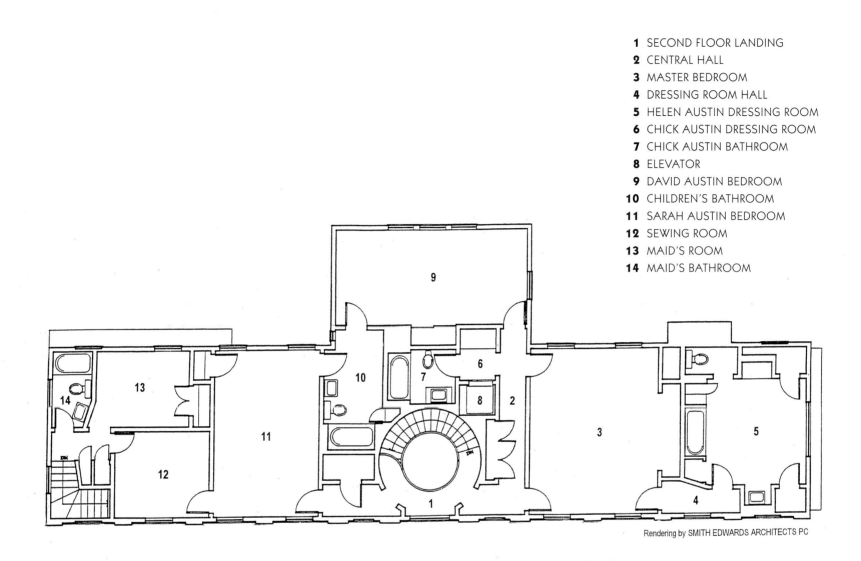

1 SECOND FLOOR LANDING
2 CENTRAL HALL
3 MASTER BEDROOM
4 DRESSING ROOM HALL
5 HELEN AUSTIN DRESSING ROOM
6 CHICK AUSTIN DRESSING ROOM
7 CHICK AUSTIN BATHROOM
8 ELEVATOR
9 DAVID AUSTIN BEDROOM
10 CHILDREN'S BATHROOM
11 SARAH AUSTIN BEDROOM
12 SEWING ROOM
13 MAID'S ROOM
14 MAID'S BATHROOM

Rendering by SMITH EDWARDS ARCHITECTS PC

ABOVE Front hall with vignette incorporating furniture and objects, brought by Helen Austin from Chick Austin's Sarasota house in 1957. Visible are a German rococo chair upholstered in a chinoiserie toile de Jouy; a painted and gilded console table from Wurzburg, c. 1740; two Bavarian soapstone sculptor's models, c. 1770; an eighteenth-century faience covered dish, and a polychrome Dutch mirror, c. 1790.

LEFT Front hall staircase showing marbleizing by Chick Austin.

ABOVE Seventeenth-century sculpture of Saint Luke, made in Antwerp, seen from the second-floor landing.

RIGHT Front passage with a Venetian mirrored door and reproduced French toile de Jouy with chinoisere design seen from the music room

ABOVE Bavarian polychrome wood clock in the form of a grotesque figure, c. 1740. Formerly in the Oscar Bondy Collection, Vienna, purchased in New York in 1949.

LEFT Music room with one of the five chinoiserie Venetian painted silk panels.

TOP German terracotta double salt dish with harlequins, eighteenth-century. Formerly in the Oscar Bondy Collection, Vienna, purchased in New York in 1949.

ABOVE Autograph score of a musical portrait of Chick Austin by Virgil Thomson, 1935.

RIGHT Music room with the Art Deco Steinway spinet purchased in 1939.

LEFT Catalogues of *New Super-Realism*, 1931, and *Picasso*, 1934, and program of *Four Saints in Three Acts*, 1934.

FACING PAGE View through the living room's carved rococo doors showing the Neapolitan Directoire settee in the music room, c. 1790, brought from Sarasota by Helen in 1957.

FACING PAGE View of the living room showing the Art Deco coffee table and the Italian settee and bergères brought from Hollywood, set against wall panels painted in Turin in the eighteenth century.

RIGHT Striped floral fabric recreated from black-and-white photographs taken in Hollywood and Hartford.

LEFT Chick Austin's portfolio from his last trip to Europe in 1956, displayed on one of his earliest known purchases – a French carved and gilded Louis XV armchair, c. 1750, owned by Queen Maria Luisa of Spain, when she was Duchess of Parma, purchased in Venice in 1926.

FACING PAGE View of the living room with the French eighteenth-century painted stone mantelpiece and Meissen porcelain figures.

ABOVE Seventeenth-century Tyrolese carved wooden sculpture of Saint George and the dragon.

LEFT Rear hall with framed German billets doux and an eighteenth-century English japanned tall clock.

FACING PAGE Dining room with the Bavarian rococo bed niche, or boiserie, and the reproduced Italian silk brocatelle in a baroque pattern.

LEFT Chick and Helen Austin's silver, crystal and china. The device on the shield reads "Agitatione Purgatur," or "It is purified by motion."

FACING PAGE
LEFT Dining room, west wall, with an eighteenth-century Venetian table from the Sarasota house and a reproduction of a Panini drawing.

RIGHT Carved cherub on the niche after restoration showing the blue and copper highlights that are reflected in the room's wall covering and carpet.

LEFT Carved and gilded Nymphenburg console table, c. 1740, with faience covered dish, Meissen porcelain figurines, Sheffield plate candlesticks. The portrait of a young girl, falsely attributed to Copley, was digitally reproduced on canvas, partially repainted and glazed, because Chick Austin had over-painted the background of the original with a lead-based yellow for a theatrical production at his Windham Playhouse.

FACING PAGE Eighteenth-century Italian carved wood, painted and gilded figures, originally intended as candle stands.

LEFT Sicilian painted and gilded commode, c. 1740, from Chick Austin's bedroom in Sarasota.

FACING PAGE Dining room showing John Vanderbank's *Portrait of an Unknown Lady*, c. 1730.

ABOVE Detail of the French toile design.

LEFT Second floor landing with the reproduced eighteenth-century French toile de Jouy curtains, looking into the north hall, revealing the children's graffiti.

FACING PAGE Master bedroom with two abstract oil paintings by Chick Austin from 1931.

LEFT Master bedroom with Genoese Louis XIV Laque and decorated commode, c. 1750, and a richly carved and gilded Venetian mirror, c. 1780, both brought from Sarasota by Helen in 1957.

FACING PAGE Master bedroom with reproduced eighteenth-century Alsatian floral toile de Jouy, showing a small framed drawing of an eyeball (*Interior Landscape*), 1944, by Pavel Tchelitchew.

FACING PAGE Helen Austin's dressing room with a Breuer stool and a digital reproduction of the original watercolor by Ossip Zadkine, 1927.

RIGHT Helen Austin's dressing room, drawers and cabinet. Like this cabinet, the closets and small bathroom duplicate the colors of the dressing room on each vertical and horizontal plane.

FACING PAGE Helen Austin's dressing room showing a Breuer stool, table and arm chair and an Art Deco drawing copied by hand from the 1930 photograph by Lisa Lichtenfels.

ABOVE Chick Austin dressing room of 1940 with scarves, boxes, and a horn, all used in his magic shows.

RIGHT Chick Austin's bathroom with his shaving mirror by Marianne Brandt, c. 1928.

GROWING UP IN THE AUSTIN HOUSE

DAVID ETNIER AUSTIN

My childhood was not that different from anybody else's in the sense that my sister and I led our own lives at the house, while all these exciting things were going on—particularly the evenings and the parties when all the artists and performers came. We weren't "presented." It was very noisy with a party in full swing, and we might look over the banisters at people down below, but we were not to be seen or heard. Mostly, I think, we weren't that interested as children. We were simply in another end of the house being normal kids to a great degree. You make your own world.

It was hard for me to see the house as strange in any way. It was just my house. But our friends would love to come over because of course it was so different from what they were used to, and there were all kinds of things that we could do. There's a river in back, and there was the high front hall. I used to make these very, very light rubber-band powered airplanes, and that was a marvelous place to fly them because they would go round and round. Someone once threw a fedora onto the head of the statue halfway up the stairs and it stayed there for a long time. And there was the corridor that runs the whole length of the house in the basement, which was a great thing for kids, because you could kick soccer balls and ride bikes from one end to the other.

For years Sally and I had a Scottish nurse, Martha Wilson—we called her Munga—who lived in the little bedroom on the north side of the house, and we both developed Glaswegian accents. We also had a series of cooks and an Italian gardener My mother liked to have breakfast in bed, so Sally and I usually ate in the kitchen and listened to the radio before going off to school.

My father wasn't around a great deal. Because he was a museum director, he spent part of the year in Europe looking at pictures and collecting pictures. Even

in Hartford, he never stood still for a moment. He would come home at night from the Atheneum and lie down on the sofa and go immediately to sleep for about five minutes, and then he would wake up, completely refreshed, and rush off to his projects at the museum or in a studio he had in Hartford. Sometimes we would all have dinner together, which was fun, but that wasn't every night by any means.

From the time I was about six years old, my mother would take my sister and me to the Atheneum quite often to see him. What I liked about these visits was that it was Daddy's museum. We all called it that. We could park our car in a tiny parking lot where nobody else was allowed to go to. His office was wonderful—a completely modern Bauhaus office, and it was his. He was the big man.

For me, the greatest thing of all was that my father used to give magic shows at Christmas time in the little theater in the museum. Of course, all my friends went to that and they just adored it. Once in a while, since my birthday is in January, I was allowed to have a magic show in our house, with maybe a dozen of my friends. My father would have all the magic boxes and paraphernalia set up in the music room, which he used as stage, while we sat below in the living room. And he did different tricks every year. He'd look for tricks in Europe—that was another priority when he went abroad—and bring them back for the new shows.

Considering that he wasn't the usual kind of father, we always had certain family rituals that meant a lot to him, especially at Christmas time, which was wonderful. We would gather together on Christmas Eve and put the milk and cookies on the mantelpiece and the usual things that you do. But there were no decorations in the living room. Then we'd be put to bed. We'd whisper for a long time and finally

Sally and David with "Munga," in Maine, c. 1939.

Sally and David on the rear terrace of the Austin House, 1952.

Helen and Chick with Sally, David, dachshund, and friends by the Park River, c. 1938.

Sally, Chick, Helen, and David traveling in Europe, 1952.

go to sleep, thinking about Santa Claus coming, and wake up in the morning and gather in the little music room overlooking the living room, with those big doors closed. My mother, who was extremely musical, would sit down at the piano and play "Once in Royal David's City," the carol, and "O Tannenbaum," one of my father's favorites, and we would sing. Then the doors would be flung open, and the living room would have been totally transformed. There was this enormous Christmas tree that reached the ceiling with the presents and the decorations, a lot of them from my father's childhood. My parents had stayed up all night to do it. That kind of ritual I think made up a lot for his absences, at least as far as I was concerned.

He had a very appealing child-like quality. He was always fun. He didn't play with us, but he was always doing things that were highly amusing to children. There was a kind of an aura about him, which I can still feel. It was imminent. It was just in the air, when he was here. I can't explain it. Other people spoke of that, too, and I know exactly what they meant.

I saw its effect even on the most obscure art dealers when we made our only trip as a family to Europe in 1952. I remember going with him to these tiny places in little towns. He would find a door—it would be a basement door to a dusty shop—and he would ring the doorbell, and the door would open and somebody would just

throw his arms around him and be so glad to see him. He knew all these little places where he could find the faience he collected—eighteenth-century French pottery—and all kinds of other objects that he wanted for his different houses in Hartford, New Hampshire, Sarasota and Provence.

As for me, my own predilections seemed to lead in a different direction, away from my father's powerful influence for a time. In fact he did not encourage me to follow in his footsteps, knowing that what he was doing was uniquely of its own historical moment and not repeatable in another context. I majored in physics in college, though at the end of my senior year at Harvard I knew I was not cut out to be a physicist. I began to think about architecture.

I had drawn pictures since I was small child. My mother particularly encouraged us in this. She had what she called the Austin Arts Club, and she and my sister and I would draw pictures and compare them. My mother was around more than my father and certainly shared his passion for art, no less than he in many ways. Although I never looked at buildings, I had a childhood obsession with airplanes and ships and was always making drawings and models of them, a skill that translated well into architecture. Also my exposure to both the eighteenth-century classicism and twentieth-century modernism, which I experienced growing up in the

Chick and David Austin, c. 1950.

David and Sally Austin, in Avery Court, Wadsworth Atheneum, November 1985.

Austin house prepared me for an appreciation of Le Corbusier, in whose work the abstract classical ideals of proportion and balance are fused with a passion for the dynamism of twentieth-century technology.

As an architect, I still marvel at the house for many reasons. One of the most important is its scale. My father saw a villa on the Brenta River, near Venice, took some pictures of it and designed this house after it. That villa is enormous. The Hartford house is small, but it feels big. It has high ceilings and each element is exactly in proportion. You can make classical architecture at any scale. If you're still using the same elements, the trick is to make them the right scale and size. For instance, the dining room has French doors. But the width with both doors open is just three feet. They're hardly big enough to get through if you only open one of them. As an architect, you begin to look at these kinds of things. You see how small the scale of the house is. But because of the proportion, it never feels that way. That was carried out beautifully throughout the house. It's eighty-six feet long, but only eighteen feet deep, and yet it has a sense of grandeur that is completely due to proportion.

Leigh French was the architect who did the plans, but I'm sure, knowing my father, that this was all he actually did. It was all custom work. Because of the scale, all the doors had to be specially made. The other thing is that my mother and father

went to Europe before they had much idea of the house and bought some interior pieces, including the boiserie in the dining room, which is an ensemble that was taken out of a house in Germany. And the living room has the baroque doors and the French mantel. He incorporated those into the house, which came later, and they fit perfectly.

Ultimately, my father's influence on my sister and me was very strong. We were surrounded by beautiful things—by art and music. Everything in the house was there for a reason. Things were either beautiful intrinsically, or studied and decided on in order to create beauty in a certain way. Some objects were very idiosyncratic, like the clock man in the music room or the plant stands that are part human in the dining room. They're strange, but then the magic he did was strange in its way. It's all a reflection of his personality. At the same time he had the eighteenth-century things, he also bought a Joseph Cornell book and a little Calder stabile. Every little detail, every picture was thought out, so that it was an aesthetic world we lived in—the sounds we heard and the things we saw. This environment encouraged us to be creative without our being conscious of it. I think creativity comes from something you're born with, but it's also a way you think, a way of using your feelings. If you were inclined in that direction, the house was a magic place.[1]

THE ANTIC SPIRIT:
MODERN AND BAROQUE AT THE AUSTIN VILLA

RICHARD GUY WILSON

Commonwealth Professor of Architectural History and Chair, Department of Architectural History, University of Virginia

The A. Everett Austin, Jr., and Helen Goodwin Austin house projects a disarmingly simple appearance: a painted wooden facade that might be mistaken for an architectural joke or a folly. But humor can mask seriousness, and the Austin villa, when created, embodied some of the most sophisticated concepts of art and architecture in the United States during the early 1930s. The house contains strong autobiographical elements, but it also questions and reconstructs ideas of modernity, historicism (ie: the use of historical styles in contemporary works), and even how art and architecture might be defined.

It was built on Scarborough Street, one of Hartford's best addresses. Helen Austin's family—the Goodwins, perhaps the city's most prominent clan—owned the land and sold it to the Austins at a considerable price. The house sits far back on its lot with a deep lawn that creates an impressive approach and also makes the structure appear diminutive and out of scale with its larger neighbors. The surrounding houses stand closer to the street, and stylistically they reference American Colonial and English medieval prototypes. In comparison, the Austin house draws upon Italian sources and resembles a Palladian-style confection. The actual model was a Veneto villa designed by Vincenzo Scamozzi in 1596. Helen and Chick Austin discovered it on their honeymoon during the summer of 1929 and photographed it. The result in Hartford was smaller in size, and built of plain pine boards. A few years later Austin had the exterior walls painted gray, but kept the white for the pilasters and trim, making the house even more striking. The façade measures 86 feet across, and 36.6 feet high at the top of the pediment, but only 18 feet deep. This, as the eminent architectural historian Henry-Russell

Hitchcock—one of Austin's close friends—observed, gave it "the quality of a backdrop on the stage."[1]

That theatrical quality continued on the interior where the small front hall with its curving staircase recalled New England Federal era houses. Austin personally mixed all the paint colors for the different rooms in the house, and here in the hall simple beige woodwork (which Austin later marbleized) complemented a travertine floor. Dominating the stairs was a late seventeenth-century statue of Saint Luke standing on a florid baroque corbel. At times other statuary and objects occupied the hall.

The hall controlled movement into the spaces on either side, such as the dining room, which was down two steps on the left. Its most prominent feature was a rococo Bavarian wooden alcove that had originally served as a bed-niche. This stood at the far end, and an over-scaled crown molding around the room added more drama. An eighteenth-century Italian silk brocatelle in a blue-green color covered the walls from floor to ceiling and was set off by a deep copper-colored carpet. The Louis XVI dining table and eighteenth-century Italian painted chairs appeared almost reticent in their simplicity against the opulent surroundings. Austin purchased these objects and many others from the Venetian dealer Adolf Loewi whose bills of more than $15,000 caused considerable anguish when Austin's mother initially declined to cover them. [2]

Similar furnishings filled the small music room on the other side of the front hall. This space opened into the living room through huge German rococo doors, and down two steps. The music room's walls were hung with framed eighteenth-cen-

Vincenzo Scamozzi, The Villa Ferretti, 1596, Dolo, Italy, 2004.

Walter Gropius dressing room, Bauhaus, Dessau, Germany, c. 1928.

tury Venetian silk panels decorated with chinoiserie motifs, which had come from Chick Austin's apartment on nearby Farmington Avenue. He had one panel left over and attached it to the ceiling. Furniture moved about the interior over the years, but normally a piano stood in one corner of the music room. The original 1930 photographs show two wildly contorted Venetian chairs on either side of a restrained and simple chest.

Spatially the two main rooms on the ground floor were laid out along sight lines where guests entered at one end as if from a stage. They would look out across the space, but would also be on view to the other guests, and then they would step down into the room. The living room measured eleven feet high. Covering the walls were eighteenth-century painted canvas backdrops in thin wooden frames. Chick made no secret of the fact that they were third-rate reproductions of older paintings of rustic maidens, buccaneers, fanciful voyages, and harbor scenes. No crown moldings were used so as not to compete with the frames of the large painted panels. Nor was there a chandelier. Light came from wall sconces, lamps and windows. A florid Louis XV mantelpiece dominated one wall and many of the furnishings were eighteenth-century Italian copies of French pieces. A variety of objects—Meissen figurines, painted boxes, silver bowls and books—stood on the tables and mantel. Covering the floor from wall to wall lay a dusty rose carpet, set off by lighter rose taffeta curtains. Beginning in the late 1940s, a low Art Deco style coffee table, covered in green leather, stood in front of an eighteenth-century Italian painted settee and matching bergères.

Against the rich coloration, texture and historical recall of the ground floor, the upstairs provided a stark contrast. The most notable space was Helen's dressing/bathroom, based on such rooms in the houses of Walter Gropius and Moholy-Nagy at the Bauhaus at Dessau, Germany. Here the brightest, and therefore the dominant, vertical color on one wall—a smooth cream—contrasted with cocoa, gray-blue, and beige on the other walls and with three lighted mirrors over a built-in dressing table. Jet-black linoleum covered the floor. The only ornamental touches were the simple metal handles and light fixtures imported from Germany. Chromium tubular furniture by Le Corbusier and Marcel Breuer completed the room when it was first seen. The simplicity and reflectivity expanded the small space.

Walter Gropius dressing room, Bauhaus, Dessau, Germany, c. 1928.

The master bedroom was equally minimalist in surface treatment with modern beige woodwork, rose walls, and a robin's-egg blue ceiling, but baroque-rococo-styled furniture gave it a surrealist air. Chick Austin's bathroom with its vibrant colors—black, blue-green, cocoa, and stainless steel—and its floating glass shelves set into the wall at one end of the tub, recalled the modernist Dutch De Stijl movement. (Austin showed an early Mondrian in 1931 at the Atheneum and later would make the first American museum purchase of one.[3]) The upstairs guest bedroom and the bar in the basement represented the more decorative side of modern design, first called "Modernistic," but later Art Deco, and furniture by Bruno Paul and Pierre Chareau helped make these spaces complete ensembles.

The house should also be viewed by reactions to it, for it attracted attention. The Hartford newspapers published long articles about it when it was completed in the late fall of 1930, and Chick Austin opened it for a day to members of the Atheneum.[4] Neighbors called it "odd," while some of the museum's trustees thought it both frivolous and pretentious: a "paste-board palace."[5] Helen Goodwin Austin's second cousin, Philip L. Goodwin, an architect whose work (with Edward Durell Stone) would include the Museum of Modern Art of 1939, claimed at the time that the modern rooms in the house represented "an entering wedge of the future," adding "when this house is old, it is very, very old, and when it is new, it is modern."[6] Somewhat later, one scholar termed it "the stage-set house," while another wrote that it was "an outrageous bit of frippery that could be blown over with one good gust."[7] Although in the 1930s any true modernist would have disparaged the copying of a Palladian villa, by the 1980s the house appeared to be prescient. One of Austin's confidants, Philip Johnson, who had led the modernist revolt, recalled his first reaction to the house with characteristic humor: "Of course none of us could stand his house. The least he could do was copy Gropius." But by 1984 times had changed, Johnson was in revolt again and declared it "a postmodern house," fifty years before the fact.[8]

The house contained a variety of opposing strains that can be variously titled the baroque, the modern and the historical. Certainly historical elements abounded, but Austin's treatment lacked the usual seriousness of most architects. Instead the house is antic, which can be defined as "odd, fantastic, grotesque," also "frolicsome, lively," or "a folly," something taken to the extreme. [9]

In a sense the Austin house resembles an English or French eighteenth-century picturesque garden structure such as the various temples, Gothic cottages and Chinese pagodas found at Stowe or Kew gardens, or Marie Antoinette's rustic Petit Hameau at Versailles. These were play houses, or stage sets, in which one could imagine another life. Chick Austin, who loved the theater and devoted much of his time to producing, designing and acting, playfully described his house as "just like me—all façade."[10]

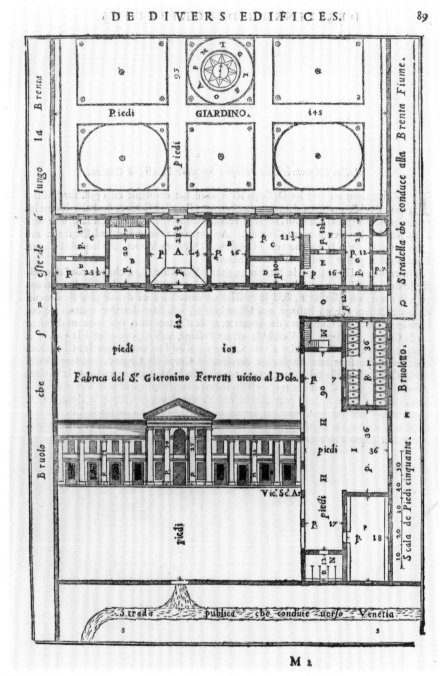

The Villa Ferretti in *Oeuvres d'Architecture de Vincent Scamozzi* of 1713.

The house contained frolicsome elements not only in the contrast of styles, the bizarre interiors, and the extreme eclecticism, but also in its details. Its source, Scamozzi's Villa Ferretti in the Veneto, was a large stuccoed building. Austin and his architect, Leigh H. French, Jr., altered the facade in both obvious and subtle ways. Typically American was the translation of European stone or stucco forms into wood and, in New England, painting them white. Austin and French used photographs and drawings of the Veneto villa, but may have looked at books by Scamozzi as well. Scamozzi (1552-1616) was a Venetian architect who worked for Andrea Palladio and completed some of his projects. Known for his stage designs—which would have appealed to Austin—Scamozzi also designed several major buildings in Venice and the Veneto and wrote a treatise on his theories, *L'Idea dell'Architettura Universale* [*The Idea of Universal Architecture*] (1615), which became a mainstay of the classical tradition. The Villa Ferretti was not published until 1713 when *Oeuvres d'Architecture de Vincent Scamozzi* appeared in Leyden.[11] Instead of the elaborate Ionic capitals that Scamozzi published in *L'Idea*, the Hartford villa's capitals are simplified and similar to the modernistic treatment of the Greco-Deco. Austin and French mimicked the fenestration pattern of Scamozzi's villa to maintain the symmetry. However, four windows in the wings of the Austin house are filled in, or blank, and they are not symmetrically placed. They create a contrapuntal rhythm; or, it might be said, an undercurrent of jazz invades the classical.

Palladianism in the form of a Veneto villa appears only sporadically in American architecture. Drayton Hall, c.1742, near Charleston, South Carolina, employs double porticos derived from Palladio's treatises. Thomas Jefferson's Monticello, in its first incarnation (1768–1782), picks up on this superimposed portico motif. His redesigned Monticello of the 1790s and early 1800s has Palladian elements such as the dome and a full height portico, but his source lay with English and French interpretations and pattern books that were based on the Veneto architect's four books. Although Palladio would remain popular for details and motifs, actual copies of Italian villas were rare in the United States.[12] An interest in the Italian garden began to appear during the turn of the twentieth century with the writings of Charles Adams Platt and Edith Wharton.[13] And Italian villa elements, though in a style pre-dating Palladio, can be seen in the work of Platt and F. Burral Hoffman of New York and David Adler of Chicago. In buildings such as Adler's Charles Pike house in Lake Forest, Illinois, 1916–1917, the emphasis lay with courtyards or piazzas and also with garden and landscape features such as terraces, walls, stairs, and statuary. Hoffman's Villa Vizcaya in Miami, 1910–1916, one of the most expensive houses of the period, was dominated by its courtyard and elaborate garden. The same could be said for Dwight James Baum's Sarasota villa for John and Mable Ringling, Ca d'zan, 1924–1926. But none of these features was important to Austin.

Drayton Hall, c. 1742, Charleston, South Carolina.

Thomas Jefferson, Monticello, 1768-1782, 1796-1809, Monticello, Virginia.

David Adler, Charles Pike House, 1916–1917, Lake Forest, Illinois.

F. Burral Hoffman, Villa Vizcaya, 1910–1916, Miami, Florida.

The closest approximation to the Austin house is found in the Georgia villas of Philip Trammel Shutze. After attending Columbia University's School of Architecture, Shutze spent five years in Rome, studying part of the time at the American Academy. While he would become known for his academic classicism, Shutze designed a few baroque villas during the 1920s. Shutze delighted in elaborate scrolled façades and

Philip Trammel Shutze, Villa Abicini, 1928, Macon, Georgia.

a wealth of highly detailed ornament as with the Dan Horgan house, also known as the Villa Albicini, 1928, in Macon, which stood out with its bold pink-reddish colored stucco contrasted with tan details. Shutze only completed about five of these very unusual baroque creations before Southern propriety—and the Depression—took hold, and he turned to the more conventional Colonial Revival.[14]

Though he was the architect-of-record of the Austin House, Leigh H. French, Jr., (1894–1946) followed Austin's directions. Chick Austin had some architectural training while at Harvard, but he needed a professional designer to work out his concepts for the house and obtain a building permit. French received some brief formal training in New York and worked for several firms before setting up his own office in the city. He designed homes for the wealthy in Ohio, Pennsylvania, and Greenwich, Connecticut. French's output recalls that of the leading country house designers of the period, such as Delano & Aldrich, David Adler and Philip Goodwin. These architects specialized in large, well-detailed country or suburban houses, which recalled Continental, English, or American colonial sources much like the other houses on Scarborough Street. Usually they were filled with high quality but restrained antiques and reproductions; and while the houses were modern in the sense of bathrooms, kitchens, and utilities, they never contained rooms that recalled the Bauhaus.[15]

French apparently did not attend architecture school, but his approach was academic, in that he followed the lead of Ecole des Beaux-Arts designers in both organized and symmetrical plans and reliance upon the accurate replication of historical forms and details. He also became known for his books and articles on early American interiors and French manor houses and gardens. His co-author on some of these publications was Harold Donaldson Eberlein, a leading historian of early American architecture. Such books provided architects with accurate photographs and drawings for use in their own work. French's measured drawings, such as those for La Lanterne at Versailles, illuminate the crispness of his approach and why he might have appealed to Austin.[16] French did the working drawings, but according to sources close to the project such as Henry-Russell Hitchcock, he "was the first to say that the house was largely of Chick's design and hardly at all of his."[17] In January 1930, shortly after construction began on the concrete basement, French and Austin parted ways. The breakup was amicable, and two years after completion a short article on the house appeared in *House and Garden* with French's name attached and the revealing title: "Baroque Curves in a Palladian House from New England."[18] Yet though the Austin villa contained historical references on the exterior and the interior, they were not the standard elements of form and detail common to other houses by French and his colleagues. Instead, the house had an air of frippery, as if it were meant to be a historicist joke.

Chick Austin's Hartford apartment, salon, with a walnut and ivory inlaid desk by J.M. Leleu, 1928

Chick Austin's Hartford apartment, study, with a desk by Pierre Chareau and a Wassily chair by Marcel Breuer, 1928.

It also stood in contrast to the new modernism emerging in American architecture. In the 1920s the zigzag or the Art Deco moderne dominated advanced architectural and interior design. Its origins lay both in America and abroad with French modernism. The work of Frank Lloyd Wright involved elaborate geometry and fractured forms, while there was also a renewed interest in Navajo and Aztec arts. The *Paris Exposition Internationale des Arts Décoratifs et Industriels Modernes* of 1925 launched a widespread international craze for the style. In the United States this approach became associated with skyscrapers and commercial construction, Hollywood movie decor, and the furniture of Paul Frankl and Eugene Schoen. A few homes were designed in the style, such as the Joseph Medill Patterson house by Raymond Hood in Ossining, New York.[19]

Chick Austin knew what came to be called Art Deco well, and in 1928, inspired by an exhibition at Lord & Taylor's department store in New York, he redesigned one of his two connecting Hartford apartments in this new style. It was typical of his eclectic approach that the traditional French and American colonial furniture in the first apartment contrasted with the Art Deco objects in the second by leading French designers such as Jules Leleu and Emile-Jacques Ruhlmann. The *pièce de résistance*

that took the visitors beyond the Art Deco was a chromium tubular Wassily chair by Marcel Breuer, one of the first in the United States. A reporter for the *Hartford Times* declared that the décor captured "the sprit of the machine age and the art represented by the modern skyscraper." Austin displayed "moral courage" with the interior and the Hartford public was admonished: "Do not fail to see it."[20]

In conjunction with his apartment's opening to the public, Chick asked Paul Frankl to lecture at the Atheneum. Frankl's line of Skyscraper furniture was among the most radical designs of the period, and his books *New Dimensions* (1928) and *Form and Reform* (1930) advocated a modernist stance. In his Atheneum lecture Frankl claimed that "simple lines are modern" and that the characteristics of the new style could be found "in the stream-line body of a car." He concluded, alluding to the dominant English exponent of the Arts and Crafts movement: "William Morris died fighting against the machine age, but the machine survived."[21] As noted above, Austin maintained an Art Deco presence in his house in the guest bedroom and the basement bar room.

By 1930 a new modernist style was emerging, the streamlined modern. In contrast to the angular or Cubist forms of the zigzag Art Deco, this design approach

Walter Gropius, Bauhaus, 1925–1926, Dessau, Germany.

favored smooth rounded surfaces that imparted—in some people's minds—a sense of speed and efficiency. Developed by the new profession of industrial designers like Norman Bel Geddes and Raymond Loewy, streamlined forms became very popular by the mid-1930s for cars and trains. Bel Geddes produced a mechanized house with a garage turntable and rounded forms for the *Ladies Home Journal* in 1931, and his book *Horizons* (1932) became a best seller. During the 1930s curving modernist forms had a major impact on the depressed furniture industry. The streamlined "moderne," perhaps because of its commercialism and the hucksterism of its champions, became the despised style among academics and the museum crowd of which Austin was a part.

The Wassily chair that Chick showed in his apartment in 1928 and the Breuer furniture in Helen's dressing room in the Austin house stood for the other major design approach that emerged in the United States in the later 1920s and early 1930s. It was known in Europe by titles such as *das Neue Sächlichkeit*, *Neues Bauen*, *Intenationale Architectur*, and "functionalism," and in the United States as the "International Style." Its leaders were the designers Le Corbusier, Mies van der Rohe, and J. J. P. Oud, along with Walter Gropius and the Bauhaus group which included Marcel Breuer. Their buildings and furniture contained simplified rectilinear geometrical forms (a few rounded shapes did appear, as in the work of Oud), a horizontal emphasis through flat roofs and banded windows, a mechanical air (Le

Corbusier's "Machine for Living"), and a messianic purpose that veered towards socialism and even communism. Another feature, and in some sense the most dramatic, especially to those brought up on the importance of decoration, was the lack of ornament in this new architecture. The avoidance of applied ornament went back to Adolf Loos's polemical 1908 doctrine, "ornament is crime." In the United States some illustrations of Le Corbusier's work appeared sporadically in magazines starting in the mid-1920s, and his first American article appeared in the *Architectural Record* in 1929.[22] His book *Vers un Architecture* appeared in an English translation in London during 1927.

Fully realized examples of this new style in the United States prior to 1930 were confined to the West Coast and the work of the Austrian émigrés, R. M. Schindler and Richard Neutra. Schindler's beach house for Dr. Philip Lovell, 1922–1926, in Newport Beach, California, easily ranks as one of the most revolutionary buildings of the decade in Europe or the United States. Although his work was widely published, Schindler remained too much an individualist for the East-Coast tastemakers.[23] Schindler's sometime partner (they had a falling out in 1927), Richard Neutra, produced the purist expressions of the new style with his Jardinette Apartments, 1927, and Dr. Philip Lovell's town house, 1927–1929, both in Los Angeles. The Lovell house or "Health House," as Neutra named it for publicity purposes, employed a steel frame that was covered by horizontally oriented glazing and thin concrete walls that gave it the air of volume rather than mass. No ornament appeared on the exterior; and the interior spaces, which flowed together on the main floor, opened to the landscape beyond.

On the East Coast the earliest examples of the new style were student projects at Harvard by Peter van der Meulen Smith, one of Henry-Russell Hitchcock's close friends, who died tragically young. Smith had worked for André Lurcat in Paris and knew the work of Le Corbusier. Two of his projects from 1927 were deeply indebted to Oud and Le Corbusier and indicate his grasp of the International Style.[24] In 1930 William Lescaze (the architect, with George Howe, of the Philadelphia Savings Fund Society in Philadelphia, 1928–1932) designed a house for Frederick Vanderbilt Field in New Hartford, Connecticut, 1931–1932, that embodied all the dictums of the International Style.[25]

Henry-Russell Hitchcock emerged as the major American proponent of this new movement, and in 1928 he actually coined the term "International Style" in an article in memory of Smith in *Hound & Horn*, the literary magazine created by Harvard undergraduate Lincoln Kirstein. Hitchcock, who studied art history as both an undergraduate and a graduate student at Harvard, was drawn to the new modernism. He wrote that Smith was "the first to bring this manner of building to our shores—or rather the first to develop an American version of what is definitely

R. M. Schindler, Lovell beach house, 1922–1926, Newport Beach, California.

Richard Neutra, Lovell house, 1927–1929, Los Angeles, California.

not a French, nor a Dutch, nor a German, nor a Russian but an international style."[26] The next year, in his book *Modern Architecture: Romanticism and Reintegration* (1929), Hitchcock tried a different term, "the New Pioneers," with reference to the advanced architecture of Le Corbusier, Gropius, Mies, Oud, Smith, and Neutra. Hitchcock advocated the new pioneers and in contrast he developed the term "the New Tradition" for architects such as Wright, Hood, and other halfway modernists and Art Decoists who still employed ornament and made reference to the past.

The term "International Style" never caught on in Europe, but by 1930 those in the know in New York, Boston and Hartford were using it. Austin became aware of it in tandem with Hitchcock. In his travels in Europe, Austin had encountered examples of the International Style, though exactly what remains unclear. But that he recognized something new was happening was obvious as early as 1928 when, shortly after returning from abroad, he told a Hartford reporter:

> The Germans realize that old-fashioned workmanship no longer exists in the new art and therefore seek to let the surface, planes, metal, and wood and glass used in homes and buildings in that country reveal their own beauty. They make shape and simplicity count for everything. The rooms, too, are shaped in modern design with ceilings in some cases fashioned in planes. I was in Germany four years ago and was surprised to discover that since that time a complete new art has sprung up there. Even the advertisements, signs on buildings, printing and the trolley cars assume the modern shape and design.[27]

Austin's knowledge of the International Style was first reflected in his remodeling of the director's office at the Atheneum early in 1930. He painted the walls and ceilings different shades of red, brown and pink. All trim was removed, and the furniture was tubular chrome by Breuer. Later that year, of course, he designed the dressing rooms at his house. During his various European trips he might have visited a house by Le Corbusier, or the Bauhaus; certainly he saw in person some of the German housing projects. The International Style was promoted and sold through black and white photographs, and while at times a sentence noted other colors the overwhelming impression was of a dry monotony. Not, however, for Austin, who used cream, cocoa, beige and blue. These rooms were among the very first East Coast examples of the new modern radical architecture.

From a larger perspective, the modern design Chick presented in his house was part of his campaign to introduce modern art to Americans. In December 1930, in a forum much more public than his house, Austin had Hitchcock give a public lecture at the Wadsworth Atheneum on the new architecture. A surprise visitor at the lecture was Richard Neutra, on his way back from Europe, who told the audience about his Los Angeles work.[28]

Henry-Russell Hitchcock and Chick Austin in front of *The Street*, by Balthus, in the James Thrall Soby house, Farmington, Connecticut, February 1940.

Widespread popular awareness of the International Style in America came in 1932 with the massive exhibition at the Museum of Modern Art (MoMA) called *Modern Architecture: International Exhibition*. It was the brainchild of another of Chick Austin's Harvard friends, Alfred H. Barr, Jr., the founding director of the Museum of Modern Art, who recruited two Harvard modern art and architecture apostles to curate it, Hitchcock and Philip Johnson.[29] In 1930, after graduation, Johnson had moved to New York and volunteered his services at MoMA. He and Hitchcock had traveled in Europe and had seen the new architecture.

The exhibition included both a catalogue, *Modern Architecture*, and an accompanying publication, *The International Style: Architecture Since 1922*, written by Hitchcock and Johnson with an introduction by Barr. Although the show contained work by Frank Lloyd Wright, Raymond Hood, and others, the thrust and polemic was that the only contemporary architecture worth considering was the white box of the International Style. Highlighted were Le Corbusier, Oud, Gropius, Neutra, and Mies and their seminal buildings such as the Villa Savoye, the Bauhaus, the Lovell house and the Barcelona Pavilion. These were supplemented with photographs, including Philip Johnson's New York apartment designed in 1930, long dis-

tance from Europe, by Mies van der Rohe at the same time Austin was building his house. Oud's major work in the exhibition was the project for a house in North Carolina commissioned by Johnson's parents but never built. Left out were individuals such as Schindler, whom Hitchcock and Johnson considered too individualistic.

Three principles underlay the new style, wrote the two authors: "architecture as volume rather than mass"; "regularity rather than axial symmetry"; and the avoidance of "arbitrary applied ornament."[30] Noteworthy in Hitchcock and Johnson's definition was the omission of a social agenda common in Europe and also modern technology.[31]

The *International Architecture* exhibition opened in New York in February 1932, attracting about 33,000 visitors and traveled to eleven cities in the next 20 months and in a reduced version appeared in various venues for the next six years. It was perhaps the landmark of all architecture exhibitions and the accompanying book has never been out of print. Between April 30 and May 28, 1932, the show appeared at the Wadsworth Atheneum.[32]

In the background of making all forms of modernism safe for Americans lay the prevailing academic tradition of the turn-of-the-century, expressed in American manifestations of the Ecole des Beaux-Arts. Painting, sculpture, decorative arts and architecture were ruled by an American Renaissance mentality that envisioned a dominant classicism, which drew upon old world or American colonial prototypes. Challenges came from the Arts and Crafts movement and also events such as the Armory show of 1913, which scandalized the public with Marcel Duchamp's *Nude Descending a Staircase*. Alfred Stieglitz's Gallery 291 showed Picasso as early as 1911, but the real change came after World War I when New York became the center for modern art with the immigration of European artists, along with the founding of the Société Anonyme by Katherine Dreier, Duchamp and May Ray, and Albert Gallatin's Gallery of Living Art.[33] Commercial galleries like Marius De Zayas, Brummer, and Daniel showed Matisse and other Europeans. Stieglitz, Edith Halpert, Richard Bach at the Metropolitan Museum of Art, and Jane Heap of the *Little Review* promoted American modern art, as did John Cotton Dana, the director of the Newark Museum, over in New Jersey. Polemical and provocative in some ways, these galleries promoted the new art as suitable for all, part of a new mainstream. You did not need to be on the avant-garde fringe to admire and purchase it.[34]

The Boston area entered this modern campaign in the later 1920s when soon after Austin left Harvard to assume the Atheneum position, a small group of students led by Lincoln Kirstein created *Hound & Horn* and the Harvard Society for Contemporary Art. They published avant-garde literature by Pound, Eliot, and others, and also showed art by Evans, Steiner, Picasso, Matisse, and the first performance of Alexander Calder's *Circus* in America. Some of Austin's watercolors were

Le Corbusier, Villa Savoye, 1928–1929, Poissy, France.

reproduced in the *Hound & Horn*, and exhibited at the Society's exhibition gallery.[35] In turn, Austin borrowed shows from the Harvard group for the Wadsworth Atheneum in 1930. These included Buckminster Fuller's Dymaxion House and works by Diego Rivera, Paul Klee, Georg Grosz, Paul Strand and Edward Weston.[36]

Making modern art acceptable to the American public was only one element in a larger reevaluation or, indeed, revolution in art history during the 1920s and 1930s. Terms such as "baroque," "rococo," and "romantic" became recognized as styles. The word "baroque" had been used originally to disparage, suggesting the grotesque or whimsical.[37] Its ultimate source lies with the term *baroco*, the Italian word for a misshapen pearl. In Italy it meant torturous, convoluted or contorted, and even false, or in artistic terms anything opposed to classical rules. In France and England baroque as applied to art meant irregular, bizarre, decadent, ugly, unpoetic, and of no real value.

Baroque as a synonym for excess and "over the top" design would persist well into the twentieth century, but a new meaning began to emerge in the 1920s. The art history faculty at Harvard played a major role in the shift of the use of the word "baroque" to a positive connotation, and also into a stylistic term. Two elements came together, first through the work and teaching of Denman Ross—from whom Austin took a class—who attempted to disembody art forms from social-cultural and religious values and see them as works of pure visual design ordered by harmony, balance and rhythm.[38] The other element was the adoption of the Germanic scientific method of formal analysis of art as pioneered by Heinrich Wölfflin and others. Wölfflin's *Kunstgeschichtliche Grundbegriffe* of 1915, though not translated until 1932 as *Principles of Art History*, was taught at Harvard by Austin's mentors Paul Sachs and Edward Forbes and at other institutions such as Princeton. Osbert and Sacheverell Sitwell and Roger Fry contributed to the rehabilitation of the baroque. The concept of the baroque as a style and a method worthy of study, on an equal footing with the Renaissance, was passed on to Austin and other Harvard art history students whose later writings and exhibitions would educate the public.[39] By 1932, the use of the word "baroque" in the *House and Garden* article on the Austin house indicated a widening acceptance of this once despised aesthetic.[40] And yet, at least to the uninitiated in Hartford, both Chick Austin and his house exemplified the pejorative definition of the word.

The creation of formal historical styles and categories would have an impact on modernism as well. Indeed, the three principles of Hitchcock's and Johnson's definition of the International Style came directly from Wölfflin's methodology. The International Style was simply one more category in the march of styles.

Although the Museum of Modern Art in New York traditionally gets the laurel as the first modern art museum, in actuality Duncan Phillips's gallery in Washington, D. C., which opened in 1921, marks the beginning. And though modern exhibitions had taken place in Chicago, Brooklyn, Newark and other locations, the Atheneum under Chick Austin's direction from October 1927 onwards is another early contender for the crown. In 1928, in addition to showing Renaissance and baroque art, he also exhibited works by Degas, Renoir, Gauguin and van Gogh (who were still considered outside the mainstream) along with Picasso, Matisse, and Derain, and the American artists Charles Demuth, Maurice Pendergast, and Edward Hopper. Some of Chick's exhibitions set fires of controversy in Hartford, but they were never fatal.

Connoisseurship did not disappear with modernism, nor did the ideal that art improved life. As Edward Forbes declared in 1925, the Fogg's educational goal was to make the fine arts "a source of joy and inspiration—an element in a life of every nation which shall work for saneness and harmony, for 'It is the love of the Beautiful that brings to order the world of the Gods.'"[41] Perhaps more prosaically, but with the same commitment, Austin spoke in 1936 of the "functions of a provincial museum" and the thread of the beautiful that ran from the past to the present, declaring that "we must have the great things of the past to enjoy and to study but with that valuable experience and pleasure as guide and criterion, we must surely seek to live in the present and to try to create the new forms which are to be our legacy to the future."[42]

With its varied interiors and motifs that stretched over three centuries, the Austin house contained autobiographical elements and could be read as a museum director's house. Chick Austin's major accomplishments at the Atheneum lay not only with his modern exhibitions and activities, but also with his championing, showing, and purchasing major examples of baroque, rococo, and other styles of art that had existed outside the canons of acceptance. He routinely combined the art from several continents and time periods in exhibitions that brought in crowds. This was part of his educational mission. Thus, in a sense, the house he created was a museum house from its conception, for it expressed his belief that seemingly divergent styles reflect the common aspirations of artists to produce new forms of beauty.

The Austin villa itself represents a particular moment in American art and design when old ideas were being questioned, adapted or swept aside. Yet while it is of its time, the house offers a challenge still valid—the challenge to experience, explore, and enjoy the arts of all times, including our own. For that reason alone, Chick Austin's house would be worthy of preservation. But it is also an essential document of the intellectual life of the 1930s. The great formers of modern American intellectual and artistic sensibilities gathered there and in many cases performed in its spaces. Above all, the personality of Chick Austin himself is indelibly imprinted on the house, as is his seminal role in the creation of American modernism. Seen in its true dimensions—which extend far beyond its deceptive façade—the Austin house is a national treasure of very great importance.

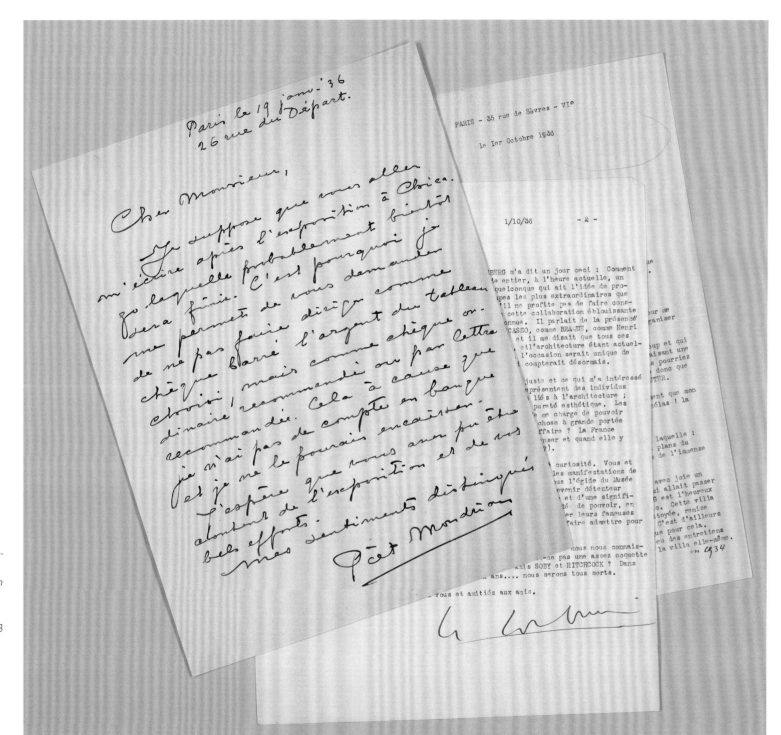

Letters from Paris: Piet Mondrian to Austin, January 19, 1935, requesting payment for *Composition in Blue and White*; Le Corbusier to Austin, October 1, 1936, offering to design a building in Hartford and declaring: "You and the Museum of Modern Art have organized the most important exhibitions of modern art in the world."

URBAN ARCHAEOLOGY:
RESTORING THE AUSTIN HOUSE INTERIOR

KRYSTYN HASTINGS-SILVER

Restoration Project Director, Lyndhurst
Austin House Restoration Project Manager, 1998–2007

In 1985 the Austin family gave the Austin House to the Wadsworth Atheneum. The house and its contents were photographed in detail, beginning the long process of documenting its history, design, collections and condition. The newly created Austin House department of the museum produced a "History, Inventory and Preliminary Recommendations" (1985) and an "Interior Architectural Survey" (1986). These were followed in 1993 by a "Conservation Survey: Overall Environmental Conditions, Furniture, Engaged Wooden Objects, and Metals" and a "Building Survey," both carried out by the Conservation Center of the Society for the Preservation of New England Antiquities (now Heritage New England). The reports, supplemented by the extensive archives of the Austin family, formed the basis of our knowledge of the Austin House. During this period, the grounds were maintained, the exterior was repaired and painted, an electrical upgrade was carried out and the original in-ground oil tank removed, and, most extensive of all, a state-of-the-art climate control system installed by the Carrier Corporation of United Technologies Corporation. After the conservation of the furnishings and decorative arts collections got underway in 1996, the museum turned its attention to a full-scale restoration of the interior under the direction of a trained restoration specialist, Krystyn Hastings-Silver.

When the process of restoring the interior of the Austin House began in 1998, the building was very much as the family had left it. The core of the museum's restoration team consisted of the Austin House Committee of the Wadsworth Atheneum's Board of Trustees, the Curator of the Austin House and the Austin House Restoration Project Manager. Although the team knew that certain deferred maintenance projects needed to be addressed, such as the exterior painting and the re-glazing of the windows, our philosophy for the rebirth of the interior was only partially formulated.

To begin, we documented the house before changing anything. The house had been photographed thoroughly in black and white immediately after it was given to the museum twelve years earlier. We videotaped each room, filming each object, and took additional photographs. We were then in a position to move the entire collection to an offsite location. Having the house empty enabled us to protect the objects and keep the cost down, because contractors could work faster when they were not impeded by objects.

Throughout the project, we maintained detailed records of all the decisions we made. No restoration team, no matter how thoroughly it has investigated the history of a house and examined the physical evidence, is infallible. There may be different opinions or a better way of looking at the building in the future. We felt that as historians, archivists, and preservationists, we had to make certain that there was a solid trail of evidence to enable those who came after us to take the house to the next level of authenticity.

Once the house was emptied we saw the opportunity to assess the layers of changes to the interior and return it to the period of greatest historical significance. We decided what that should be by studying the history of the house and Chick Austin.

Chick Austin had originally hired an architect from New York, Leigh H. French, Jr., to translate his sketches and photographs of the Villa Ferretti into the

ABOVE Exterior wall repair.

RIGHT Installation of piping for
the new sanitation system.

Two views of Helen Austin's dressing room, 1985.

finished house. Chick chose him because he was knowledgeable about historic European villas and had adapted the designs of them for new American houses. But French did not stay to see the job through to completion. Chick not only oversaw the final construction of the house, but also the interior decoration. Completed in 1930, the house immediately became both his home and his stage set for entertaining. Knowing that, it was clear to us that for the interior, the focal period encompassed the years 1930 to 1943, the year Chick left the Atheneum on a leave of absence, followed by his resignation. The exterior changed with the addition put on the back for an extra bedroom in 1940, which is also when the Austins painted the house a warm gray color.

What we learned led us to the philosophical decision, as a committee, to restore the outside to the early 1940s and to bring the interior envelope back to the 1930s. And when we said "envelope," we meant the walls, the ceilings, the curtains and the textures, because the objects were transient in Chick's time and continued to be so during his and Helen's occupancy together. An example of that is the vignette in the entry hall; we view it as Helen's tribute to Chick because she brought objects from his Sarasota home and placed them in similar settings in the Hartford house, which is clear from photographs that she had commissioned after Chick's death in 1957.

With our underlying philosophy in mind, working with the Society for the Preservation of New England Antiquities (SPNEA) and the preeminent fabric

Austin House living room, 1985.

Austin House dining room, 1985.

house, Scalamandré, we began to go through the Austin House and look for the evidence that would support what we wanted to accomplish. We already had contemporary photographs and descriptions. When the house was finished in 1930 it was such an unusual building that Chick and Helen opened it to the members of the Atheneum under the auspices of the museum. The negatives from the rotogravure article about the house in the *Hartford Courant* that came to the museum with the family archives provided us with views of the primary spaces as they were originally conceived. The house also appeared in a 1932 *House and Garden* article. We had family letters and snapshots, and the Austin children, David and Sally, shared their memories of the house. When we had a phase of

the restoration finished or had a decision to make about a fabric or a color, we would invite David to visit and ask him: "Does this feel right?" One of the most gratifying moments came when we had restored the living room. David walked in and saw the room as it was in the 1930s with the original colors and the reproduced curtains and carpets. He told us that he had come home in a profound sense. He stood in the middle of the room and said, "This is just the way it was when I was a child."

There were also boxes of fabric in the attic and a great deal of physical information throughout the house. It was rather like putting a jigsaw puzzle together as we figured out where all the pieces belonged. We had to find ways to connect col-

105

LEFT Chick Austin's Sarasota house, front hall, showing rococo chairs, console table, faience covered dish and Bavarian sculptures, moved to Hartford in 1957.

FACING PAGE Austin House rear exterior after restoration, with reproduction of 1930 garage doors, 2000.

ors and fabrics described in contemporary sources to what we had in hand and what we uncovered beneath the surface.

An example of that came from the dining room. The 1932 *House & Garden* article had mentioned a copper-colored carpet in addition to the stunning blue-green silk walls. When the museum acquired the house, the dining room had been untouched since a 1950s redecoration, which included the addition of an inferior parquet floor and new wall coverings. We believed that the original carpet was completely gone, and we did not know what was meant by "copper." But we were very fortunate. I pulled up the floor myself, and under the wooden threshold of the interior French screen doors

leading to the terrace I found a piece of the original copper carpet, which had been used as a shim. It was not water-soaked, and it had not deteriorated to a point where it was impossible to see the right color within its wool pile. We were able to give that sample to Scalamandré, and they reproduced a carpet that matched it.

As a part of the same parquet-floor demolition, I removed the baseboards and discovered behind them a piece of the original silk wall covering. It ran behind the base molding to where it met a door casing. It tapered down and we could see the tack marks from Chick's installation and how he literally stretched it between the two pieces of wood without any gimp edging. Because he purchased this as an

Silk thread reproduction for the blue-green brocatelle in the Austin House dining room on the loom at Scalamandré's mill, Long Island City, New York.

Remnant of the original brocatelle discovered behind the dining room baseboards.

Original and reproduced brocatelle with enlargements of the 1930 photograph of the dining room.

Discovery of the remnant of the original copper-colored carpet under the threshold of the French doors leading from the dining room to the terrace.

Conservation and restoration of the Bavarian bed niche by conservators from SPNEA, 1996.

antique fabric from a dealer in Venice, he had only a limited amount to work with, and he covered the raw, uneven edges with the wood trim.

With remnants of the original fabric in hand, we made the decision, in keeping with the Department of Interior's standards, to replace it with the same or better material. We had the fabric reproduced to the exact scale and color, then had it mildly distressed to suggest an antique origin. We had a cropped and enlarged view of one corner of the room from the first photographs, showing that there were places where the fabric was misaligned or patched, but we agreed that if Chick could have done it correctly the first time he certainly would have. We elected to install it as it would have been if enough fabric had been available in 1930.

We found confirmation of the dining-room colors on the rococo alcove that constitutes one wall. Conservators from SPNEA carried out detailed studies of the inte-rior surfaces of the house, as well as conserving some of the architectural elements, furniture and decorative objects. They felt that it was Chick who had applied turquoise and copper paint to the wood paneling of the alcove to reflect the colors of the textiles he chose for the room.

We returned to the original photographs repeatedly. Restoration work often focuses on one element at a time and it is easy to overlook many other details, so we continued looking to see what we might have missed, whether it was a little didactic object or something as obvious as the frosted light bulbs.

Every paint color in the house is a custom mix, and discovering those original colors was an adventure. The walls in the music room and living room were lined with canvas, which was typical of the period, to hide hairline cracks, but the

Samples of the original paint in the rear hall.

Conservation and restoration by Susan Buck of the eighteenth-century japanned English tall clock carried out on site due to its fragility.

house had been re-canvassed in the 1950s, so physical evidence existed only on the woodwork and behind the switch plates. In other spaces, we were fortunate enough to find a clean sample large enough for the SPNEA conservators to analyze, and then we would try to match it.

That happened in the back hall. The colors exposed through the layers of paint on the walls and trim were two shades of an unlikely warm yellow. The evidence was absolute so the paint was applied, but with trepidation. We should not have doubted Chick. He had taken effects of light into account, for the yellow is transformed into the perfect transition color between the dining and music rooms. The 1930 photograph of the south wall of the dining room allowed us to see, through the open door to the back hallway, dark silk curtains with a soft valance. We deduced that the curtains had been a wine-red color because Chick had painted the inside of the bathroom door across the hall from them that color. The door had been removed in 1974, but Helen had stored it in the basement. Because of its fragility, the japanned eighteenth-century tall clock in the back hall was restored at the house by an SPNEA conservator.

The music room was a great challenge. The 1930 black-and-white photographs showed us that from a tonal standpoint this room was not the dark avocado green

that it was in 1985. But no extant paint was visible. The original Venetian panels of dark gold silk were still affixed to the walls and ceiling. Chick had moved them from his apartment on Farmington Avenue and used them to set the tone for the space. The frames of the panels were streaked with Chinese red, and through cracks in the painted surface of the green paint on the moldings around the doors and windows, we could see similar red streaks on a gold background. The SPNEA conservators were able to confirm those colors by gently unveiling other trim areas with paint solvents, which revealed a dark creamy gold color. We were hesitant, however, to choose a color for the walls through guesswork or surmise. We found some samples on the unfinished wood floor when we removed the carpet that reminded us of a Jackson Pollock painting. We could see all the mixing that was taking place, but no one color dominated, so we set the decision aside. Then I noticed that one switch plate was cut and tucked behind the decorative wall trim. I pried it loose and found a two-square-inch fragment of the original linen canvas that had been painted the tawny gold that Chick had created in 1930. Once we had the document, our master painters were able to match it. That, in turn, led us to believe that a tiny piece of gold silk in a small box that Helen had stored in the attic was a remnant of the curtains. We found a very similar fabric in Scalamandré's line and had the curtains

Krystyn Hastings-Silver conserving the frame of a silk panel in the music room.

RIGHT Sample application of wall and woodwork paint colors to match original colors revealed near the bottom of the molding.

reproduced, providing a luxurious but unobtrusive complement to the room.

I think of this as urban archaeology.

The dusty rose wool carpet that ran from the back hall, through the music room and into the living room had been recycled to the main staircase when the family made the major changes to the interior decoration in 1950–1955, but it was so faded we could not match it until we examined a segment from the staircase that had been folded and tacked and therefore untouched by sunlight. Scalamandré reproduced it from the sample.

Finding the wall color in the living room was even more difficult than in the music room. We had descriptions of a dark green from the 1930 newspaper article and the *House & Garden* article two years later, but we could not even begin to guess the precise shade. I removed the hardware from the windows and then the windows themselves to look for original paint, but fragments of pigment were too small to be used as a basis for color reproduction.

We knew from the 1930 photograph that before Chick marbleized the stairs leading down into the living room in 1950, they were the same tone as the base molding. I pulled the carpet back and found the color that we thought we needed. But it was terribly scuffed and had variations on the surface, so we were still not certain.

RIGHT Sample application of possible living room wall paint colors.

BELOW Living room doors partially closed revealing a section of a wall with the 1950s paint color.

We had the painters apply six rectangles of different intensities of the same sort of blue-green across a section of the wall. Those samples made it clear that Austin was using a combination of the colors in the sea and skies featured in the large painted panels that formed the backdrops for the room. But which was the right one? We viewed the six samples on a cloudy day and a sunny day and at night with artificial light. On a Tuesday morning we made the decision and had a large section of one wall painted. It went so well with the panels that we felt that it had to be the correct choice. Days later, we were vindicated when we discovered that the color we had chosen, and named "Tuesday," perfectly matched a paint color that had been in full view all the time. Chick had applied it to the grooved molding of the mirror frame over the mantelpiece. When the walls and woodwork were repainted a yellow green in the 1950s, the frame of the mirror had been left untouched. Once again, as with the alcove, Chick had tied the room's colors together and had left us clues.

Our admiration for Chick's skill as a colorist increased with each room. It was important to remember that in the summer and fall of 1924 Chick trained in Siena,

Fabric samples for curtains, upholstery, and carpet in the living room.

Chick Austin's Hollywood house with Italian settee and matching bergères, upholstered in the original striped floral fabric, c. 1947.

Italy, with Federigo Ioni, who was known as the "King of Forgers." That was where Chick learned techniques of mixing tempera paints, for which he displayed a distinct talent. Besides touching up the historic decorative elements that he used, he also painted the frames for the Venetian silk panels in the music room and the Turin canvases in the living room, making them appear to be originals.

To proceed with the furniture and fabrics, we had to learn the story of the living room. We came to recognize that the panels, painted by a journeyman artist in the manner of Claude Lorraine, were both a backdrop and a palette for Chick. Just as the sky and sea of the paintings inspired the wall color, the two-toned work surround is the misty rose of the curtains and the dusty rose of the carpet. The upholstery colors were drawn also from various elements in the panels.

The Venetian suite of furniture—the sofa and two bergères—was purchased in Hollywood when Chick spent a period of time there in the mid-1940s. The pieces were subsequently reupholstered, and we had no fabric remnants to guide us, only black-and-white photographs. They showed how the designs in the material came

Italian bergère after the suite was moved to Hartford, c. 1949.

RIGHT Eighteenth-century French painted stone mantelpiece with reproduction mirror panes.

BELOW Chick Austin's dining room, Sarasota, with candelabra, chandelier, and console table moved to Hartford by Helen in 1957.

forward or receded depending upon the light, but for the colors we relied on David Austin's memories and what we now knew of Chick's decorating tricks. Scalamandré produced sample skeins based on their vast experience with classic French fabrics and on mock-ups we made from paint chips. The final version has the same sheen as the original and the colors pair beautifully with the panels on the wall behind. For the other furniture and the curtains in the living room we were able to use fabrics that were in production.

Chick brought the Art Deco table covered in green leather to the house from Hollywood in the late 1940s and placed it in front of the Venetian suite. He knew that even though these pieces were from very different periods, they would complement each other. The table is very low, like the suite, and the flare of the legs has the feeling of the chinoiserie style that was so popular in eighteenth-century Europe.

We had to replace the panes in the mirror over the fireplace which were originally mercury glass, but we found a company that could match our sample and distress the new panes to a fine facsimile. The Meissen porcelains on the mantel were held together with Scotch tape. They were yellowed, pieces were missing, they had been repeatedly repaired, and they were filthy. We had them restored following contemporary conservation practices for porcelain, making a clear distinction between what was infill and what was not.

Helen brought the chandelier in the living room back from Sarasota after Chick's death. Although it was not present during the period of greatest significance, we decided that it should remain for several reasons. It tells more of the story of Helen's incorporation of objects from the Sarasota house into the house in which the family had lived together. It matches the original sconces over the mantel. The children remembered that Helen had always wanted a chandelier in the room. And, happily, she had it wired to a separate circuit so that it could be turned off to recreate the more atmospheric ambient light of the 1930s.

The small passage between the music room and the front hall was wallpapered in 1974, but we found odd-shaped bits of old chinoiserie red toile in the attic. When we laid them out we saw that they had been cut to cover exactly all the areas of exposed wall in the space, even the narrow strips surrounding the eighteenth-century mirrored door mounted there. We also had the accompanying gimp. Although we wanted to restore the fabric to the walls, we did not have enough to identify the repeats. Then we had another serendipitous discovery. The textile collection at the Atheneum had a complete sample of the very same fabric, called *Pantagruel in the Silver Isles*, which we used as the basis for our reproduction.

In the front hall we made one of the major exceptions to our decision to bring the interior envelope back to the 1930s. We retained and restored the marbleized

Restoration of the travertine floor, Austin House front hall.

Paint sample of the original beige wall and woodwork color,
discovered under the carpet on the staircase in the front hall.

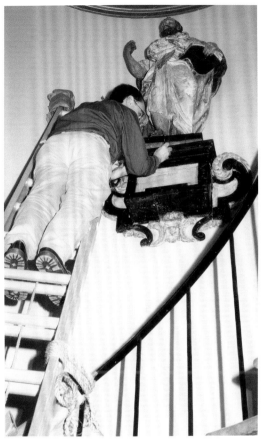

SPNEA conservator Keith Bakker
distressing the paint surface of
the Saint Luke sculpture after
initial restoration.

trim. Around 1950 Chick enlisted his son David and his niece Jane Goodwin to help him create the faux marble surface, and we could not possibly obliterate his hand. The marbleizing was part of the evolution of the space and typical of Austin's theatricality.

The travertine floor in the hall was dark, dingy, and chipped. We brought in a team that specialized in the restoration of floors and surfaces. They replaced areas of loss with color-matched infill, repaired the grout and sealed the floor with a water-based protective product that would be our sacrificial upper layer, especially during the winter when people might bring in sand and salt on their shoes in spite of the large hemp door mat. Travertine goes back to Roman times, and Le Corbusier used it in a number of his buildings. This was a reminder of Chick's propensity to use materials with a "past-meets-future" aspect. There is a subtle vocabulary

throughout the building, and after years of discovering Chick's decorating methods, one could recognize his thought process.

The statue of Saint Luke mounted in the stairwell was restored in place using scaffolding because there was too much potential for damage in taking it down. An expert in polychromed wood from SPNEA cleaned it, touched up the gold pigment and also replaced a part of the saint's lip, which had fallen off, and one of the edges around an eye. We wanted a very small amount of in-painting on the base, without improving upon the condition at the time Chick bought it. When the work was finished, however, we compared it to the 1930 photograph and thought it was too perfect. The conservator agreed to return and willingly distressed his own work. This was a situation in which we had to rein in a conservator and find a happy medium between restoration and authenticity.

FAR LEFT Discovery of the 1940 wallpaper in the hall to Helen Austin's dressing room.

LEFT Original eighteenth-century toile de Jouy curtain panel and a curtain panel from the 1960's redecoration.

The staircase and second-floor hall provided us with a "eureka moment." We pondered the colors, working from the December 1930 prints taken for the newspaper article. We could judge the values of the walls and carpet, but we did not know the colors. Then one morning I was sitting on the stairs talking with the curator and an architect on the Austin House Committee. I was about to remove the old rose carpet, and I mused aloud that there must be something to tell us about the colors. As I spoke, I pulled up the carpet and there, as if I had planted it, was a scrap of the original dark blue carpeting that had been reused as padding. The wall color was

a less dramatic discovery. We knew that the walls and woodwork were originally the same color and that when Austin added the marbleizing, he treated only the edges of the stairs and risers. As we removed the carpet, the original sandy beige color of the woodwork, and therefore the walls, was fully revealed.

The upstairs hall along the master bedroom wall was restructured in 1940 when the addition was built onto the back of the house for David's bedroom. Because of that, we decided to cover the walls with the dark brown geometric paper that Chick installed at that time. Scalamandré reproduced the paper from a large segment discovered behind a bookcase. We believed that the original 1930 curtains for the central Palladian window—a blue and beige toile in an eighteenth-century design—were still in place when the new hall was first papered. These curtains were replicated by Scalamandré, and we further treated them with a tea bath to achieve an appropriately mellow tone.

The dome completes the illusion of grandeur in the entry hall. It is the only calcimine ceiling left in the house. Because of the fragility of the surface and its relative inaccessibility, we decided not to disturb it. The light above it, which produces a lovely theatrical effect at night, is actually an ordinary screw-base, type-A light bulb in the attic, in a socket with a piece of aluminum flashing wrapped around it in a conical shape. It reflects and distorts the light and gives the feeling that the glass is something more interesting than it actually is. Securely mounted on a beam above the dome is an air conditioning unit from the Carrier Corporation, the central component of our museum-quality climate-control system.

When we removed the wallpaper from the north hallway, we uncovered a lively piece of childhood graffiti in pencil from 1948. Above and below two views of an ocean liner, carefully drawn by David, were twelve-year-old Sally's angry scrawls aimed at her brother, along with other sibling doodles. We felt very strongly about preserving these drawings because of their interpretive value. They illustrate that the house was not only a showcase for entertaining the luminaries of modernism, but also home to a family with children who could ignore the baroque and the Bauhaus. It was just where they grew up.

Chick's dressing room is smaller than it was in 1930 because of the later reconfiguration of the hallway. We decided that the anteroom would be an appropriate place to display samples of the magic paraphernalia that Chick had used as "The Great Osram." The space also gave us an opportunity to display some of Chick's personal items, including an array of towels from several periods, each monogrammed with "AEA." Helen had stored them in the attic, laundered and pressed.

By working down through the paint layers in Chick's bathroom, we found that each plane of the walls had its own color. The darkest shade is on the wall above the very stylish tankless toilet. The color no longer served its original purpose because the window on that wall had disappeared in the 1940 addition. Above the sink opposite is one of the Bauhaus light fixtures that we had replicated from the 1930 photographs, and alongside it is Chick's circular, lighted shaving mirror, a 1928 design by Bauhaus artist Marianne Brandt. Sally Austin had taken it to her

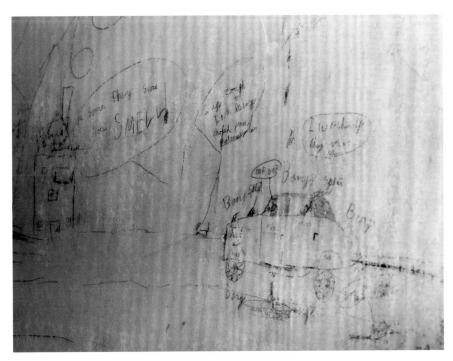

Detail of graffiti by Sally and David Austin in the second floor hall, c. 1948.

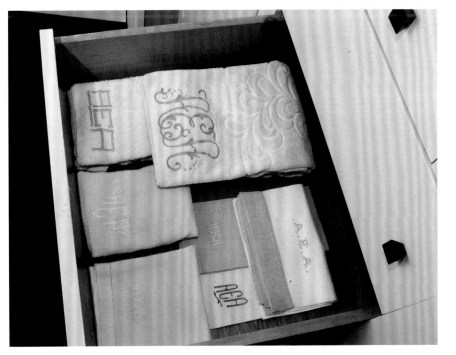

Chick Austin's monogrammed towels in a drawer in his dressing room.

Snapshot of David Austin in his parents' bed, c. 1939, showing the original Alsatian toile de Jouy.

A sample of the original Alsatian toile de Jouy.

summer house in Maine, but returned it when the Hartford house came to the museum. David told us where it had been attached to the wall, and we installed it to accommodate a man of Chick's height—five feet, eight inches, as recorded in his 1935 passport.

The floor was another happy surprise. We did not have a photograph that showed the 1930s flooring. But shoddy workmanship has its rewards for the urban archaeologist. When I peeled away the later sheet vinyl, there were small fragments of the original flooring left by the installers along the corners. It was the same glossy jet-black linoleum with a jute backing that had been in Helen's dressing room—a very avant-garde and cutting-edge material for Hartford—and it was restored.

Our ideas for the master bedroom evolved during the course of the restoration. At first we were going to use it for a didactic meeting space, but as we progressed, we realized we could make it the most personal space in the house.

We had identified and repainted the surface colors—flat beige and rosy pink walls with a robin's egg blue ceiling—before we understood them. As with other areas, we decided to wait for evidence that would explain Chick's choices. Then we

came across two very small, two-by-three-inch photographs from 1937 of David in his parents' bed. They revealed that the headboard and curtain behind the bed niche were covered in a classic Alsatian floral fabric with peacocks called *Bois de Loire*. I had already found boxes of that very fabric in the attic, labeled "Mr. and Mrs. Austin's bedroom." At the time, we could not decide whether the drapes, valences, bedspread and odd cuttings even belonged to the house. They might have been used at one of the Austin houses in Maine or New Hampshire, but I recognized the bookshelves flanking the bed in the photograph, identifying it as the Hartford house, and everything came together. Chick drew all the colors in the bedroom from the fabric. The pattern was available in Scalamandré's line and we had it reprinted in the colors of the Austins' material. For formal photography and other special occasions, the original 1930s bedspread is used on the bed. The master bedroom was one of the few places in the house where we could show the contrast between decades-old and reproduced material.

We filled the shelves with books from the more than fifty boxes of the Austin family library stored in the museum's Archives, and completed the room with

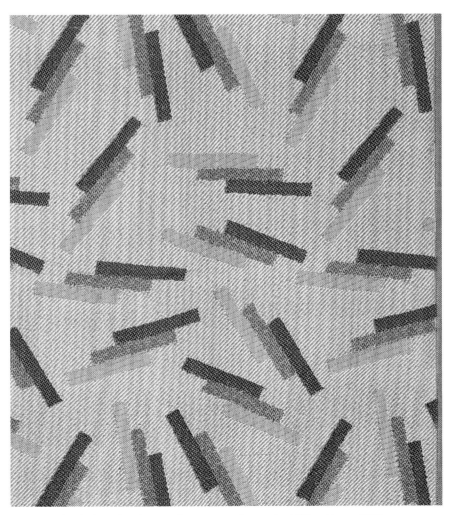

Broken sticks, designed and woven in cotton and rayon by Hélène Henry, 1927.

Installation of the black linoleum in Helen Austin's dressing room.

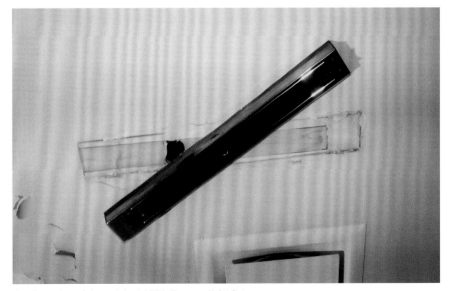

The footprint of the original 1930 German light fixture,
revealed under the 1940s American replacement fixture.

furniture that Helen used through the years. On a nineteenth-century mahogany desk, we arranged a display from a large collection of her personal objects that she left with the house when she moved to a health-care facility.

The small hallway leading from the bedroom into Helen's dressing room presented us with another mystery. The only image we had of the space was in a 1930 photograph of the dressing room. It showed us a small section of the wall covering reflected in the mirror over the dressing table. It looked like paper, but when we enlarged the photograph, we found that Chick had applied an Art Deco fabric over the plaster. We later found evidence of tack marks. But we could not determine the colors. Did they relate to the dressing room? Were there four different colors in the fabric that corresponded to the colors of each wall? It was too great a leap to make such an assumption, so we left it alone.

In the meantime, I had set up a file on the Internet to alert me to any new design books related to the periods represented in the house. After several years, the fabric appeared on the cover of a new book, *Art Deco Textiles*, by Alain-René Hardy. The fabric was called "Broken Sticks" and was created by Hélène Henry in 1927. She wove her own fabric, so it was produced in limited quantities. It is likely that Chick and Helen bought it in Paris in 1929 on their honeymoon, when they were acquiring other fabrics for their future house. Rather than have it rewoven, we had a facsimile digitally reproduced on a cotton sateen.

Helen's dressing room was actually the first room we restored. When the Austins gave the house to the museum, the room had long been altered. The walls were painted cream, the floor covering was a vinyl composition tile, and the German International Style tubular light fixtures had been removed and discarded during the Second World War. We knew from 1930s articles in the Hartford newspapers that the colors had been beige, cocoa, cream and blue, and we could see the different tone values in the photographs, but we did not understand the extreme execution of the elevation-by-elevation treatment until we began excavating through the paint layers with a sharp scalpel. Chick used the same rules, on the larger canvas of this dressing room, as he had in his own bathroom. Again, each surface facing the same direction is the same color, including the interiors of the closets, the drawers and even the edges of the doors. The painters almost resigned because of this until they began to appreciate the artistic mind at work.

The horizontal surfaces are also locked into the pattern. The plane of the floor is the high gloss, jet black linoleum; the dressing table is black; the horizontal surfaces inside Helen's built-in cabinets are black; and the wooden seat of the tubular stool in front of the windows is black.

The mirror adds to the story, as well. When we were researching Marcel Breuer, we examined photographs of the Bauhaus at Dessau, Germany, which included images of the house of the school's founder, Walter Gropius. The three-sided mirrored niche was taken straight from that house, as were the horizontal toggles of the light switches, the square brass drawer pulls, painted black, the plane of the doors, and the door handles. Chick was clearly familiar with what came to be called the International Style through his own trips to Germany and information supplied to him by his close friend, the architectural historian Henry-Russell Hitchcock. Chick borrowed the vocabulary of the Bauhaus and felt free to adapt it to his house.

We arranged the furniture to match the 1930 photographs as closely as possible. The Breuer armchair had disappeared. We used instead a similar Breuer piece that Chick had purchased for the Atheneum's new Avery building in 1933. We replaced a much later black canvas on the chair with a reproduction of the original blue Eisengarn fabric, created in four colors at the Bauhaus in the 1920s. The canvas and chrome Breuer stool at the dressing table had also disappeared and, again, we replaced it with a different Breuer stool bought for the museum in 1933. The table is a reproduction of the original Breuer table, authorized by the Bauhaus Museum. The lost Art Deco drawing to the right of the windows was replicated by an artist from the photograph. We extrapolated the dimensions of the light fixtures from their footprints, which were still visible on the ceiling and walls, and from the photographs, and had them reproduced.

The dressing room was treated differently from most other spaces in the house. Whereas downstairs the objects are not static and may change within their envelope, this room is finite in its presentation because of its historical significance. Although it may be refined in certain ways, it is stripped down to its minimalist creative moment, which is how the room was originally meant to be experienced.

In the course of the overall restoration of the house, we worked with talented conservators and representatives of more than thirty-six trades. We met with them initially to explain our philosophy and ascertain that they could work within our parameters. We were fortunate to have such a skilled team of people who could realize our vision. We also had collegial relationships with the city inspectors whom we brought in early on the project. They appreciated our taking the time to explain the museum's goals for the house and gave us the flexibility we needed to achieve them.

We have tried to bring an extraordinary American house, and the important moment in time it embodies, back to life, true to a great creative personality, his family, and their taste. It is not we as a committee, or a curator, or a donor who dictated the way in which the house should be restored. Rather we let the house dictate to us. That has been our approach—to follow the physical evidence left behind. We let the house tell its own compelling story, the Austin story.[1]

NOTES

ABBREVIATIONS

AEA   A. Everett Austin, Jr.
DEA   David Etnier Austin
HGA   Helen Goodwin Austin
SGA   Sarah Goodwin Austin
AP   Austin Papers, Wadsworth Atheneum Archives

THE STAGE-SET HOUSE

1   *Hartford Courant*, Dec. 17, 1930.
2   Claude Lorraine, *Port de mer au soleil couchant*, 1639, collection of the Louvre, Paris..
3   Elaine Moynihan Crucius, recorded interview, July 20, 1999, WA Archives.
4   A. Everett Austin, Jr., *The Artful Rococo* (Sarasota: The John and Mable Ringling Museum of Art, 1954), pp. 2-3.
5   *Hartford Courant*, Feb. 6, 1931.
6   *Hartford Times*, March 15, 1930.
7   Ibid., Dec. 17, 1930.
8   *Hartford Courant*, Dec. 17, 1930.
9   William Cole in conversation with the author, c. 1990.
10   John Gay in conversation with the author, 2001
11   Ralph Childs, recorded interview, May 1986, WA Archives.
12   *Variety*, Jan. 22, 1936.
13   Virgil Thomson, "The Friends and Enemies of Modern Music," in *A. Everett Austin, Jr.: A Director's Taste and Achievement* (Hartford: Wadsworth Atheneum, 1958), p. 62.
14   AEA, "The Undergraduate Library," n.d., AP.
15   Sir Osbert Sitwell, "Foreword" in *A Director's Taste*, p. 15.
16   *Hartford Courant*, Nov. 21, 1934.
17   Francis Goodwin II, recorded interview, Jan. 9, 1975.
18   "AEA's introduction [of] Mr. E. Krenek," typescript, Dec. 12 [sic], 1938, AP.
19   *Hartford Times*, Dec. 12, 1928.
20   Adolf Loewi to A. Everett Austin, Jr., April 4, 1933, AP.
21   *Hartford Times*, March 15, 1930.
22   Henry-Russell Hitchcock, "A Everett Austin, Jr., and Architecture" in *A Director's Taste*, p. 39.
23   Ibid.
24   AEA, "The Baroque," *1950 Art News Annual*, Vol. XIX, p. 12.

25   Agnes Mongan, recorded interview, July 21, 1983. After Austin's death Miss Mongan wrote that she and her colleagues all had a way "of wondering whenever we saw a baroque painting, if it was a picture that Chick would pass, if it would meet his standards of quality. His flair, knowledge & courage have influenced his whole generation & through us the taste of the country." Agnes Mongan to HGA, May 1, 1957, AP.
26   AEA to Philip Goodwin, April 1, 1930, AP.
27   AEA to Philip Goodwin, June 12, 1930, AP.
28   AEA to Philip Goodwin, July 11, 1930, AP.
29   In 2007 dollars, the total cost was just under one million dollars.
30   Margaret Kimberly Wood in conversation with the author, April 1, 1992.
31   David Austin, recorded interview, June 17, 1997, WA Archives.
32   SGA, recorded interview, Feb. 2, 1992, WA Archives.
33   *New York Sun*, Feb. 1984.
34   Carl Van Vechten to Gertrude Stein, Feb. 8, 1934, in Bruce Hellner, ed., *The Letters of Carl Van Vechten* (New Haven: Yale University Press, 1987), p. 134.
35   Julien Levy, *Memoir of an Art Gallery* (New York: G. P. Putnam's Sons, 1977), p. 142.
36   Alexander Calder and Jean Davidson, *Calder: An Autobiography with pictures* (Boston: Beacon Press, 1969), p. 146.
37   Kirstein's private diaries, hitherto unavailable, reveal that Balanchine's first masterpiece in America, *Serenade*, though listed in the program for the second night, was not performed because the dress rehearsal was unsatisfactory. See Martin Duberman, *The Worlds of Lincoln Kirstein* (New York: Alfred A. Knopf, Inc., 2007), p. 272.
38   *New York Herald Tribune*, Dec. 20, 1934.
39   Gertrude Stein, *Lectures in America* (Boston: Beacon Press, 1985), pp. 59, 78-79.
40   Eugene Berman, "Legendary Chick" in *A Director's Taste*, pp, 48, 50.
41   Ibid., pp. 48-49.
42   Le Corbusier, *Quand les cathédrals etaient blanches: voyage au pays des timides* (Paris: Librarie Plon, 1937), pp. 129-30. Citation translated by ERG.

43   AEA, Director's Annual Report for 1935, typescript, WA Archives.

44   Virgil Thomson, *Virgil Thomson* (New York: Da Capo Press, 1966), p. 251.

45   Paul Bowles, *Without Stopping*, (New York: Echo Press, 1985), p. 190.

46   Paul Cadmus, recorded interview, July 8, 1996, WA Archives.

47   HGA to Marie-Claire Tonny, March 10, 1938, copy in AP.

48   David Austin in conversation with the author, 1999, and Sarah G. Austin, recorded interview, Feb. 12, 1992, WA Archives.

49   SGA, recorded interview, Feb. 12, 1992, WA Archives.

50   AEA, "Annual Report of the Director, January, 1942," WA Archives.

51   AEA to Truda Kaschmann, [Aug. 13, 1943], AP.

52   Alfred H. Barr, Jr., to AEA, [June] 1944, AP.

53   David Austin in conversation with the author, March 11, 2005.

54   *Sarasota Herald-Tribune*, March 2, 1952.

55   AEA to James and Eleanor Soby, Sept. 2, 1950, AP.

56   *Sarasota Herald-Tribune*, March 31, 1957.

57   A. Hyatt Mayor to HGA, [April 12, 1957], AP.

58   Florence Berkman, recorded interview, March 27, 1990, AP.

59   Stephen Calloway, "The Baroque and the Modern," lecture at the Wadsworth Atheneum, Oct. 4, 2000, audio recording, WA Archives. The confluence of modernism and the revival of the baroque-rococo in twentieth-century Europe and America is brilliantly illuminated by Stephen Calloway in his monograph *Baroque Baroque: The Culture of Excess* (London: Phaidon Press Limited, 1994).

60   Stephen Calloway, *Baroque Baroque*, pp. 61-62.

61   After A. L. Rowse, the poet and well-known Shakespeare scholar, met Helen and saw the house, he published a perceptive poem called simply "Chick Austin." (A. L. Rowse, *A Life, Collected Poems* (Edinburgh: William Blackwood, 1981), pp. 260-1). Virgil Thomson, Henry-Russell Hitchcock and Angela Lansbury were among the distinguished friends who visited Helen into the 1970s.

62   Philip Johnson, recorded interview, Nov. 30, 1982, WA Archives.

63   Philip Johnson, recorded lecture, Avery Theater, Wadsworth Atheneum, Feb. 25, 1984, WA Archives.

64   Lincoln Kirstein to Eugene R. Gaddis, Jan. 11, 1985, WA Archives.

65   Board of Trustees, Wadsworth Atheneum, "A Resolution in Honor of Helen Goodwin Austin, Sarah Goodwin Austin and David Etnier Austin," Nov. 21, 1985, WA Archives.

66   Rowe also said that "as the visual document of an important artistic personality, I can only think that it is to be placed, *not* alongside the house of Sir John Soane in London, but—*at least*—alongside the house of Giorgio Vasari at Arezzo and the studio of Eugene Delacroix in Paris. . . ." Colin Rowe to Eugene R. Gaddis, Sept. 13, 1985, WA Archives. In one of the many other expressions of gratitude to the Atheneum, Genevieve Harlow Goodwin wrote: "I am so glad that you are restoring it. . . . Thanks to you, people all through the years will be able to admire it and think of his planning so much for others." Mrs. James L. Goodwin to Eugene R. Gaddis, Sept. 5, 1987, WA Archives.

67   AEA, fragment of a typescript for a lecture [1936], AP. The lecture was most likely "Modern Design," delivered at the Cooper Union in New York on May 7, 1936, *Hartford Times*, May 9, 1936.

GROWING UP IN THE AUSTIN HOUSE

1   Based on interviews with ERG, Nov. 27, 1990; June 17, 1997, and with Connecticut Public Television, February 22, 2001. Revised by David Austin, 2007.

THE ANTIC SPIRIT

Research assistance for this article has been provided by Krystyn Hastings-Silver, Lydia Brandt, and especially, Eugene R. Gaddis.

1   Henry-Russell Hitchcock, "A. Everett Austin, Jr. and Architecture," in *A. Everett Austin, Jr.,: A Director's Taste and Achievement* (Hartford: Wadsworth Atheneum, 1958), p. 39. In 1958 the Austins made an addition to the rear of the house. In addition to references below, see: Nicholas Fox Weber, *Patron Saints: Five Rebels who Opened America to a New Art 1928-1943* (New York: Knopf, 1992).

2   Eugene R. Gaddis, *Magician of the Modern: Chick Austin and the Transformation of the Arts in America* (New York: Knopf, 2000), pp. 117-118.

3   Gaddis, *Magician*, pp. 144-45, 284.

4   "400 see Exhibit…" *Harford Times* Dec. 17, 1930; "400 Admire Exhibitions of Austin House," *Hartford Courant*, Dec. 14, 1930.
      "400 Admire Exhibitions of Austin…" *Harford Courant*, Dec. 17. 1930.

5   William Cole, quoted in Gaddis, *Magician*, p. 119.

6   Philip Lippincott Goodwin, *Rooftrees: The Architectural History of an American Family* (Philadelphia: J. B. Lippincott, 1933), p. 61.

7   Winslow Ames, interview, 1974 quoted in Gaddis, *Magician*, p. 119.

8   Philip Johnson, lecture at Wadsworth, February 25, 1984, quoted in Gaddis, *Magician*, p. 124.

9   *Oxford Universal Dictionary*, 3rd ed. Revised (Oxford: University Press, 1955), p. 75.

10   Ralph Childs, recorded interview, quoted in Gaddis, *Magician*, p. 124.

11   Vincenzo Scamozzi , *Oeuvres d'Architecture de Vincent Scamozzi* (Leyden, 1713), 89; see also, Franco Barbieri e Guido Beltramini, *Vincenzo Scamozzi, 1548-1616*, (Venezia: Marsilio, 2003), pp. 356-359.

12   Richard Guy Wilson, "Palladio Redux," in *Building by the Book 3*, ed. M. di Valmarana (Charlottesville: Center for Palladian Studies in America, University of Virginia Press, 1990), pp. 53-87.

13   Charles Adams Platt, *Italian Gardens* (New York: Harper and Brothers, 1894); and Edith Wharton, *Italian Villas and Their Gardens* (New York: Century Company, 1904).

14   Officially some of Shutze's work was done under the firm name of Hentz, Reid, and Adler. See: James Grady, *Architecture of Neil Reid in Georgia* (Athens: University of Georgia Press, 1973): Elizabeth Meredith Dowling, *American classicist : the architecture of Philip Trammell Shutze* (New York: NY : Rizzoli, 1989); and William R. Mitchell, *J. Neel Reid: architect of Hentz, Reid & Adler and the Georgia school of classicists* (Savannah: Golden Coast Pub. Co., 1997).

15   Adler's interiors, sometimes done by his sister Francis Elkins, or Syrie Maugham have modernist features, but never the extreme of Austin.

16   Among French's solo publications are: *Colonial Interiors: Photographs and Measurer Drawings of Colonial and Early Federal Periods* (New York: W. Helburn, 1923); "Correct Pro-

portioning of Rooms," *House and Garden* (November 1928), pp.82-3; Triptych, *Architectural League of New York Yearbook and Catalogue* (1920), p.30. He is the joint author on the following: Harold Donaldson Eberlein and Cortlandt van Dyke Hubbard, *Colonial Interiors, Federal and Greek Revival*, 3rd Series (New York: W. Helburn, 1938; Harold Eberlein and Roger Wearne Ramsdell, *Small Manor Houses and Farmsteads of France*. With an introduction by Leigh H. French, Jr. (Philadelphia and London: J.B. Lippincott Co.; New York: the Architectural Record Co., 1926); House of Madame de Pompadour, Versailles," *Architectural Record* (October 1923), pp. 321-328; La Lanterne, Versailles, Seine-et-Oise," *Architectural Record* (May 1923), pp. 431-450; "Numéro 93, rue Royale, Versailles," *Architectural Record* (March 1923), pp. 245-263; "Numéro 147, Boulevard de la Reine, Versailles," *Architectural Record* (Sept.1923), pp. 277-285; "Octroi, Barriere, Porte Louveciennes, Versailles; House, no. 16, rue d'Angouleme, Versailles," *Architectural Record* (June 1923), pp. 551-561; "Pavilion de Madame, Versailles," *Architectural Record* (July 1923), pp.79-93; "La Ranchere, Saint Nom-la-Breteche, Seine-Et-Oise," *Architectural Record* (April 1923), pp. 307-316; "Saint Vigor, Viroflay, Seine-et-Oise," *Architectural Record* (February 1923), pp.116-134; *Smaller Houses and Gardens of Versailles from 1680 to 1815* (New York: the Pencil Points Press, Inc., 1924); "La Villa Trianon, Versailles," *Architectural Record* (August 1923), pp.177-187.

17   Hitchcock, "A. Everett Austin, Jr.," p. 39.

18   "Baroque Curves in a Palladian House from New England," *House and Garden* 62 (November 1932), pp. 38-9.

19   See Robert A. M. Stern, *Raymond Hood* (New York: Institute for Architecture and Urban Studies and Rizzoli, 1982), pp. 78-79; and Walter Harrington Kilham, *Raymond Hood, Architect* 105 (New York, Architectural Book Pub. Co. 1973). Among the many studies see Karen Davies, *At Home in Manhattan: Modern Decorative Arts, 1925 to the Depression* (New Haven: Yale University Art Gallery, 1983); and Richard Guy Wilson, Dianne Pilgrim and Dickran Tashjian, *The Machine Age in America* (New York: Abrams, 1986).

20   Dorothy Verrill Yates, "Modernist Apartment Is of Unique Beauty," *Hartford Times*, Dec. 12, 1928.

21   "Hartford to Take its first look at Modernist Furniture," *Hartford Times*, c. Dec. 10, 1928; and "Modernist Home Exhibit Planned," *Hartford Times* Dec. 6, 1928.

22   *Architectural Record*, Aug. 1929.

23   Among the many writings on both individuals, see David Gebhard, *Schindler* (London: Thames and Hudson, 1971); Michael Darling, Kurt L. G. Helfrich, Elizabeth A. T. Smith, Robert Sweeney, and Richard Guy Wilson, *The Architecture of R. M. Schindler* (Los Angeles: Museum of Contemporary Art, and New York: Abrams, 2001); and Thomas S. Hines, *Richard Neutra and the Search for Modern Architecture* (New York: Oxford University Press, 1982).

24   Searing, "International Style: the crimson connection," *Progressive Architecture* (Feb. 1982), pp. 88-91.

25   Christian Hubert and Lindsay Stamm Shapiro, *William Lescaze* (New York: Institute for Architecture and Urban Studies and Rizzoli International Publications, 1982).

26   Hitchcock, "Four Harvard Architects," *Hound and Horn* (Sept. 1928), pp. 41-47.

27   "Atheneum Plans Interesting Year," *Hartford Times*, Aug. 24, 1928; also, "Plans Exhibit of Furniture at Atheneum," *Hartford Courant*, Aug. 25, 1928.

28   "Hitchcock Lecture to Illustrate Modern European Architecture," *Hartford Times*, Dec. 13, 1930; "Architecture is Topic for Today's Talk," *Hartford Courant*, December 15, 1930.

29   Sybil Kantor, *Alfred H. Barr, Jr. and the Intellectual Origins of the Museum of Modern Art* (Cambridge: MIT Press, 2002).

30   Henry-Russell Hitchcock and Philip Johnson, *The International Style* (New York: W. W. Norton, 1932), p. 20.

31   Barr in his introductions to both the catalogue and the book, mentioned the technological aspect, but Hitchcock and Johnson's approach employed the new German art historical methodology that attempted a visual classification system. Needless to say, the concept of architecture in the service of a social revolution would not have gone down well at an institution like the Museum of Modern Art, funded by the Rockefeller family.

32   "Exhibition of Modern Architecture," *Bulletin of the Wadsworth Atheneum* (April 1932), pp. 13-16.

33   Jennifer Gross, ed., *Société Anonyme: Modernism for America*, (New Haven: Yale University Press, 2006).

34   Kristina Forsyth Wilson, "Exhibiting Modern Times: American Modernism, Popular Culture, and the Art Exhibit, 1925-1935." Ph.D. dissertation, Yale University, 2001; William S. Lieberman, ed. *Art of the Twenties* (New York: Museum of Modern Art, 1979); and Susan Noyes Pratt, *Modernism in the 1920s: Interpretations of Modern Art in New York from Expressionism to Constructivism* (Ann Arbor: UMI Research Press, 1985).

35   Austin's watercolors *La Cimiteria: Venice* and *The Old City: Carcassonne*, were reproduced in the *Hound and Horn* (Jan.1928), p. 228. See also, Leonard Greenbaum, *The Hound and Horn, the History of a Literary Quarterly* (The Hague: Mouton, 1966); and Mitzi Berger Hamovitch, ed., *The Hound & Horn Letters* (Athens: University of Georgia Press, 1982).

36   Gaddis, *Magician*, pp. 139-141.

37   *The Compact Edition of the Oxford English Dictionary*, p. 170.

38   Marie Ann Frank, "The Theory of pure design and American architectural education in the early twentieth century," Ph. D. dissertation, University of Virginia, 1996.

39   For historiograph, see Michael Podro, *The Critical Historians of Art* (New Haven: Yale, 1982); entries on "Baroque Art" in *Encyclopedia of World Art* (New York: McGraw-Hill, 1971), Vol. 2, pp. 28-64; Erwin Panofsky, "Three Decades of Art History in the United States, in his, *Meaning in the Visual Arts* (New York: Doubleday Anchor, 1955), pp. 321-346; C. T. Carr. "Two Words in Art History I. Baroque," *Forum for Modern Language Studies* (April 1965), pp. 175-190.

40   Stephen Calloway, *Baroque Baroque: The Culture of Excess* (London: Phaidon Press, 1994).

41   Edward W. Forbes, "The Campaign for a New Museum," *Fogg Art Museum*, II (April 1925), pp. 23-24, 28, quoted in Gaddis, *Magician*, p. 54.

42   AEA, typescript, [1936], AP.

URBAN ARCHAEOLOGY

1   This essay is based on a recorded tour of the Austin House by Krsytyn Hastings-Silver in two sessions during 2006. It was edited and amended by Ann Brandwein for this publication.

ACKNOWLEDGMENTS

The Wadsworth Atheneum expresses sincere gratitude for the generosity of those who made this publication possible: William D. Eppes, the principal sponsor, a long-time admirer of Chick Austin, who proposed the undertaking; the Felicia Fund, with special thanks to Pauline C. Metcalf; Furthermore, a Program of the J. M. Kaplan Fund, with particular gratitude to Joan Kaplan Davidson; and James B. Lyon of West Hartford, the first Chairman of the Austin House Committee. The accompanying exhibition, which shares the title of the publication, was wholly sponsored by the William and Alice Mortensen Foundation of West Hartford. We are extremely grateful for this generous support, with particular thanks to Robert S. Carter, Jr.

This book and the exhibition at the Wadsworth Atheneum mark the culmination of more than two decades of research and restoration that have brought a unique American landmark, its creator, and his circle of artistic arbiters, back to life.

The preservation of the Austin House became possible through the great generosity of the family of A. Everett Austin, Jr.—Helen Goodwin Austin, David Etnier Austin and Sarah Goodwin Austin—when they accepted the Atheneum's invitation to entrust their house and its collections to the stewardship of the museum. Their cousin Genevieve Harlow Goodwin provided a munificent endowment to make their historic gift possible. We are forever grateful to these gracious and foresighted donors, whose family members were among the founders of the Atheneum and Hartford itself.

Among subsequent benefactors of the Austin House, Melinda Martin Sullivan, a chairman and longtime member of the Austin House Committee, and her husband Paul Sullivan have been without equal in their leadership, their affection, and generosity. We thank them very warmly.

The Carrier Corporation, a subsidiary of United Technologies Corporation, generously provided the Austin House with a completely new climate control system. We are especially grateful to Harry Gray, former Chairman and Chief Executive Officer of United Technologies, for proposing this critical improvement and to his successor, George David, for bringing the project to fruition

We remember with heartfelt gratitude five exceedingly supportive donors to the Austin House who are no longer with us: Eleanor Howland Bunce, Dorothy C. Archibald, Elizabeth Gengras, the Reverend Charles Goodwin (in memory of Charles A. Goodwin), and Henry Sage Goodwin.

Indispensable grants to the museum came from several agencies, foundations, and individuals: The National Historical Publications and Records Commission; the Henry Luce Foundation; the J. Walton Bissell Foundation; and the National Trust for Historic Preservation, through its intern program, sponsored by *Yankee Magazine*. These made possible the organization of the Austin Papers in the museum's archives along with detailed studies of the house, its history and architecture. Melinda Sullivan generously sponsored conservation and architectural surveys by the Society for the Preservation of New England Antiquities (SPNEA), now Heritage New England, which in part resulted in the designation of the house as a National Historic Landmark. Subsequently, the Institute of Museum Services provided a grant for the conservation and restoration of furniture, decorative objects and engaged architectural objects by SPNEA's conservators. We thank architect

Jared Edwards for initiating and helping us implement much of this preparatory work and with his firm, Smith Edwards, for providing a conceptual plan for the restoration.

Many corporations and businesses were generous to the museum during the project. Foremost among them was Scalamandré, the New York fabric house. We express deep thanks to Adriana Scalamandré Bitter, Chairperson, Robert F. Scalamandré Bitter, Co-President, and their talented staff, especially Liana Zandomenego, Trish Connolly, Julie Kaminska, and Ed Goodman. Through them, we recaptured the colors and textures of Chick Austin's original setting with stunning accuracy. We are very grateful to Kathleen Coville Marr, a former chair of the Austin House Committee and an excellent interior decorator, for facilitating our work with Scalamandré and identifying many other superb artisans, and for her aesthetic guidance.

We thank Forbo Flooring North America of Hazelton, Pennsylvania, for donating all of the jet-black linoleum for the International Style dressing rooms and bathrooms on the second floor.

We are grateful to Mickey Cartin, a former Atheneum trustee and a distinguished art collector, for leading us to Lite Makers, Inc., of Long Island City, New York, who created exact reproductions of the original German chromium-plated lighting fixtures.

We express appreciation to the following: Adaptive Textiles of West Chester, Pennsylvania, for providing an outstanding photographic reproduction on cotton of the Art Deco fabric in the hall adjacent to Helen Austin's dressing room; Metzger's Lighting of West Hartford, Connecticut, for recreating the original ambience of the 1930s; Jim Reiner, owner of Mayflower Laundry & Dry Cleaners in West Hartford, Connecticut, for donating the services of his company in artfully tea-staining two of Scalamandré's fabrics; and Karen Lough at Upholstered Walls and Decorating of New York, for fabricating and installing curtains, wall-coverings, and bed-hangings. For bringing Chick Austin's personal color palette back to light, we thank the superb artist-painters of Sans Painting & Decorating of Vernon, Connecticut: Leo Sans and his two sons, Matt Sans and the late Michael Sans.

We express our gratitude to all the other companies, contractors, merchants, artisans and individuals whose work was carried out to the highest standards, and whose names are permanently on record at the Austin House.

We give special thanks to Robert H. Smith, Jr., and the late William G. DeLana; the late Carol Dean Krute; Susan Chandler; the late Katherine S. Hoffman; conservators Keith Bakker, Susan Buck, Mary Lou Davis, Patricia Garland, and Sarah Nunberg; Joe Gallinato of Imperial Decorating and Upholstery; Beryl Whitmore; Ray Christensen; Alain-René Hardy; the Musée des arts décoratifs et du textile; Stephen Calloway; Lisa Lichtenfels; Ashley McDonald; Dudley Rockwell, Joan Burdge, and Florence LaPorte; Martin L. Obando; John Scott Rodgers, the antique silver and clock specialist; David Morton; Ellen Wicklum; Alexander R. C. Rower; George P. Lynes II; Antony Penrose; the Harvard University Art Museums; the Yale Music Library; and the John and Mable Ringling Museum of Art.

The museum's Board of Trustees, the Austin House Committee, Honorary Committee, and Advisory Council have been of immense value for their enthusiasm, wisdom, and hard work. Each of the chairs has contributed to the success of the Austin House in distinct and special ways. We sincerely thank all the members of the committees and the council.

During the past twenty-two years, the Atheneum's directors and the staff of every department of the museum have been immeasurably helpful with all aspects of the Austin House. We thank every one of them, past and present, along with many talented interns.

The restoration of the Austin House would not have been brought to its splendid conclusion without the knowledge, the astounding ability to absorb new information, the organizational skills, the energy, the devotion to historical accuracy, and the good cheer of our Restoration Project Manager, Krystyn Hastings-Silver.

We thank the present members of the Austin House Committee, wisely chaired by Duffield Ashmead IV, for their enthusiastic support of this publication. The museum is especially indebted to Angela Lansbury for setting the scene so vividly with her own memories of Chick Austin. We thank David Austin for his personal reminiscences of growing up in the house. We are deeply grateful to all the other contributors: Richard Guy Wilson for placing the Austin House in the context of twentieth-century culture and American domestic architecture; Krystyn Hastings-Silver for presenting her account of the restoration with great immediacy; Ann Brandwein, the museum's Assistant Archivist, for her insightful editing and invaluable service in every phase of our work on the house; Geoffrey Gross for his exquisite new photographs that brilliantly capture the atmosphere of the house; Allen Phillips, the Atheneum's Collections Imaging Manager, for translating with matchless artistry all of the images into the handsome illustrations printed by Hitchcock Press; and interns Tara Sweeney and Meghan Ray. It has been an enormous pleasure to work with the designer of this book, Abigail Sturges, whom we thank for a beauty and elegance entirely worthy of its subject. We thank, too, Enid L. Zafran of Indexing Partners, for her deft and rapid contribution. Finally, we express our gratitude to the staff of the University Press of New England, the distributor of this book, for their kind encouragement and assistance.

EUGENE R. GADDIS

AN APPRECIATION

William D. Eppes has long been a patron of the arts and education. He initiated this publication with a telephone call and an offer of support. He had met Chick Austin only once, at the Ringling Museum, in the late 1940s. Knowing of Austin's interest in motion pictures, he had written for an appointment to confer about promoting a foreign film series that he was showing at schools and colleges in the Saint Petersburg area. Austin immediately invited him to Sarasota, and Mr. Eppes found their meeting intensely memorable. "Mr. Austin was on the terrace, sitting at a small table, cocktail in hand. (I was surprised—a public building, you know.) It was CinemaScope. He was in a director's chair with the sun setting over his shoulder, and David—the big bronze copy of Michelangelo's David—was out there behind him in the background. He was an absolute charmer. I remember his eyes so well—he had these penetrating blue eyes, and he looked at you and really listened as if you were the most important person in the world. When he turned it on, he was up to one hundred watts and over. He was unforgettable."

Mr. Eppes followed Austin's career closely in the press afterward and visited the Austin House when much of the restoration was completed. As a descendant of Thomas Jefferson, he was well acquainted with historic houses, particularly those with Palladian elements, and felt that the Atheneum should have a book that would present the Austin House to a wider public. The museum is deeply grateful for his enthusiasm and generosity.

PHOTOGRAPHY CREDITS

INDEX

Italic page numbers indicate photographs.

I.N.
f15